C000259666

On Your Bike
Northamptonshire

❊

Stephen Dyster

COUNTRYSIDE BOOKS
NEWBURY, BERKSHIRE

COUNTRYSIDE BOOKS
3 Catherine Road
Newbury, Berkshire

To view our complete range of books,
please visit us at
www.countrysidebooks.co.uk

ISBN 978 1 84674 030 5

Designed by Graham Whiteman
Cover photo shows Arthingworth

Photographs by the author
Maps by Gelder Design & Mapping

Produced through MRM Associates Ltd., Reading
Typeset by CJWT Solutions. St Helens
Printed by Cambridge University Press

CONTENTS

THE ROUTES

INTRODUCTION

Small in size, passed through by major transport routes, with one tip in the fens and the other almost touching the Cotswolds, Northamptonshire is a county quite wrongly ignored by the tourist. Her monuments are the stately home of the aristocrat, the manor house of the squire, the ancient church and chapel, the deserted village of the medieval peasant, the red-brick boot and shoe town, the ironstone cottages of numerous villages, the broad expanses of land that were once royal forest. The great castles of Fotheringhay and Northampton are gone – with Rockingham still standing high above the valley of the River Welland. The battles that were once fought against Vikings and the civil strife of the Wars of the Roses and the English Civil War have passed away. The boot and shoe industry and the iron and steel works have come and largely gone. Today the towns are expanding and major roads tear across the county. For the cyclist, the product of this is a shire at the heart of England, a network of quiet roads and the unexpected around the corner.

The landscape undulates, with three great river valleys and numerous smaller ones mixing with hills to give fine views. The highest – and steepest – hills are in the west and north: in the east and south they are gentler. Yet even at their worst the hills are never long, compared to many parts of Britain: the views per foot climbed are excellent value! The fit cyclist will find few of the hills daunting, but the puff-challenged rider should feel no shame in getting off and pushing. And there is always the descent to look forward to.

As far as possible, the routes in this guide are along country lanes. Where main roads have to be crossed, and there is no convenient bridge or crossing, great care must be taken, although, where a busy crossing is used, then an alternative has been given. Where stretches of bridleway or byway have been used, they are all suitable for a road bike, though clearly not for one with racing tyres. Suitability for children is really a matter for parental judgement: avoid the busy crossings and select sections or routes likely to be within the capability of the rider.

The routes are intended to introduce the rider to this fine county. There are plenty of opportunities to explore, and I hope the book guides you to some of the delights of this county of 'squires and spires' and encourages you to look around the corners and go off the beaten track.

Stephen Dyster

GUIDE TO USING THIS BOOK

Cycling should be a pleasure – and it can be, whatever your level of fitness, whatever the time of year, and whatever bike you are riding. The important thing is to have a suitable bike, dress sensibly, be prepared, and not stretch yourself until you are up to it.

Each route in this guide is preceded by information about:

Distance: only you can decide which is best for you. Where possible a range of distances has been given.

Introduction: this gives a general idea of how strenuous the route is and of places passed through, with some information about the area. Details of places of interest on or near the route are given at the end of the route description.

Maps: a sketch map showing the route is provided, but an Ordnance Survey map for the area is highly recommended and gives more ideas for extending or shortening routes.

Refreshments: pubs and cafés are indicated. This is not an exhaustive list, and remember that not all public houses are open all day. Indeed, sad to say, there are sometimes permanent closures. If you are dependent on a particular refreshment stop, then it may be best to check it out first. The Highway Code states clearly that you should not ride a bike under the influence of alcohol or drugs.

Places of interest: this is a personal selection, and you may find other things of interest along the route. The information is up to date at the time of writing, but it may be wise to check it out before your visit.

Routes: you may find it useful to read the whole chapter before setting out, in order to note places to stop and alternative routes. Directions such as **turn L** at the T-junction are given in bold; carrying straight on is not. T-junction means one where you give way to traffic on the road you are joining. Signposts have been referred to: these are usually reliable but occasionally they have been removed or tampered with. Not all the place-names on every signpost are given. However, a bit of commonsense should see you through. A starting point is given, but you can, of course start at any point on the route. Public transport is not very useful for getting around Northamptonshire carrying a bicycle, so most routes have a car park at the start but, where there is not, please respect others and park sensitively.

FOR NEW OR INEXPERIENCED CYCLISTS

Give yourself plenty of time to ride and look round. There is no shame in regular rests and the odd push – leave racing to the racers. Remember that the more you cycle, the fitter you will become and the miles will roll by more easily.

TRAFFIC

Follow the Highway Code, signal clearly, and show the consideration for other road users that you would like them to give to you. When approaching walkers and horse-riders from behind, warn them that you are coming. I generally give a friendly greeting from forty or fifty yards, rather than sneaking up behind and making them jump. This is especially important when overtaking horses. Even the calmest horse can be spooked by a bicycle, leading to all sorts of dangers – not least you getting kicked.

Take care when crossing busy roads. The routes in this book usually use bridges or crossing points with traffic lights. Where they do not, just be patient and, if necessary, dismount.

No attempt has been made to assess suitability for children. Road sense and confidence in traffic are important factors as these are not traffic-free routes. Moreover, age, experience, confidence and strength vary a great deal, and only you can assess those but, to start with, it is best to err on the side of caution. Consider places free of traffic (for example in Salcey Forest or the Brampton Valley Way) and build skill and confidence before venturing out on to roads. Cycle training courses are often available through schools or local authorities and are an excellent way to introduce children to road riding.

YOUR BIKE AND WHAT TO CARRY

These routes are suitable for most types of bike. The few off-road sections are on generally good surfaces or are avoidable. Make sure your bike is comfortable and in good working order. Check it before a ride: brakes, gears and tyres, and carry a basic tool kit and spares. In particular a spare inner tube, a pump that works and fits the type of valve on the inner tubes, tyre levers, puncture repair kit and a pair of long-nosed pliers. If you do not have quick release wheels you will need a spanner to undo the nuts. Before you set out, it might be a good idea to check that they are not fixed too tightly! Unless you are very unlucky you will get few punctures, but do remember when repairing one that you should check the tyre inside and out to ensure that whatever caused the puncture is not still in there.

A saddle-bag will have plenty of room for all this gear, as well as snacks or a picnic. Some cyclists use rucksacks but be aware that, unless it is a proper cycling rucksack, it can put extra strain on the back, unbalance the rider and obstruct vision when manoeuvring. A bottle of water should be carried, especially in warm weather. A bottle cage is easily fixed to a bike, so you don't have to get off to drink, although you might prefer to have a ready excuse to enjoy the scenery.

You should carry lights. The law on these is currently under review but, at the time of writing, it is likely to become lawful to have flashing lights on a bicycle. However, for a front-light on unlit roads you will need a light that casts a beam. Be visible to other road users!

CLOTHING

Lycra shorts are excellent for cycling, but they are not to everyone's taste. Avoid shorts or trousers that will rub, especially denim or anything too baggy. Clothing should be light in colour. Consider reflective jackets, even during daylight, and certainly at night or at dusk. Be ready for rain and, in winter, take extra layers of clothing. Gloves are very useful – a lovely downhill freewheel on a sunny spring morning can be surprisingly chilly on exposed fingers. The shoes you wear will depend on the type of pedal you have. The sole needs to be thick and relatively stiff. Thick socks are important in winter – and, if it is wet, a spare pair can make life much more pleasant at the end of the ride.

According to the law at the time of writing, you do not have to wear a helmet when cycling. It may help protect your head in a fall, but only if it is worn properly. Do not be lulled into a false sense of security: if you are run over by a steam-roller it will not help.

AREA MAP SHOWING THE LOCATIONS OF THE RIDES

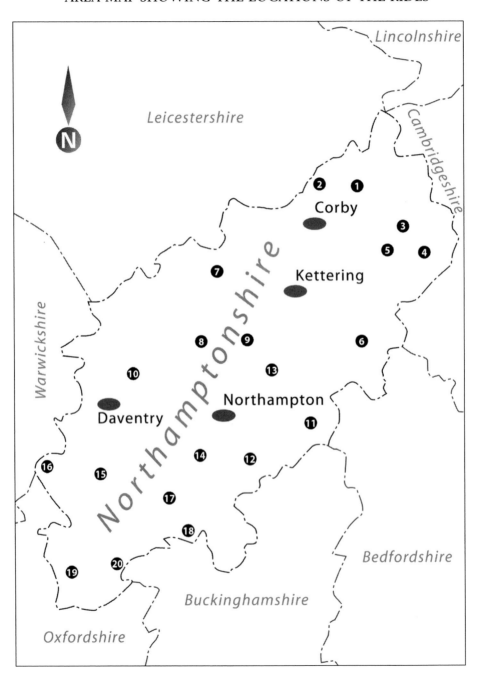

1

Bulwick, Deene Park and Kirby Hall

9 miles or 12 miles

In the heart of Rockingham Forest, one of Northamptonshire's former royal forests, this short ride around the valley of the Willow Brook passes through pretty villages such as Bulwick, Blatherwycke, Laxton and Deene, with mellow stone houses and an abundance of flowers lining the village streets. All are good places to sit and admire the surroundings. Deene Park was the home of the Brudenell family, whose most famous son was the Earl of Cardigan, who rode at the head of the Light Brigade as it charged the Russian artillery at the Battle of Balaclava during the Crimean War. Kirby Hall, a grand Renaissance mansion, is one of Northamptonshire's gems. Blatherwycke, where a stately hall once stood, sees the little Willow Brook flow under a bridge to form a lake: the second lake to be filled by this stream, the first being at Deene Park. It fills another at Apethorpe Hall, a little further downstream.

Map: OS Landranger 141 Kettering and Corby (GR 962942)

Starting point: Although there is no car park in Bulwick, where this route starts, the road into the village from the A43 is wide enough to allow roadside parking. However, if you wish to visit Kirby Hall, you could start from there (GR 925928). Bulwick is signposted off the A43 between Duddington and Corby. Kirby Hall is reached by turning off the A43 at the sign for Deene and then following the signposts. The nearest railway station is at Stamford, some 10 miles of hilly road away.

Refreshments: The Queen's Head, just off the A43 in Bulwick (telephone 01780 450272), is an attractive old roadside inn. Although there is no tearoom at Kirby Hall, the friendly reception staff will sell you tea, coffee, ice cream and such like.

The route: This relatively short route uses a fairly peaceful stretch of the A43 for a hundred yards or so. The rest is all on minor roads and a track near Kirby Hall. There are several undulations along the quiet lanes, but nothing too strenuous.

Starting in Bulwick, with your back to the church, go left up the village's main street. Soon **turn L** (Blatherwycke/King's Cliffe), and follow this quiet lane to Blatherwycke, swinging to the left over the bridge. Shortly after, **turn L** (Laxton/Harringworth). This narrow lane, part of the national byway, reaches the A43 at a crossroads. Go straight on (byway). At the T-junction, **turn R** (Laxton/Harrington). Swing past the large green in Laxton and follow the road out of the village.

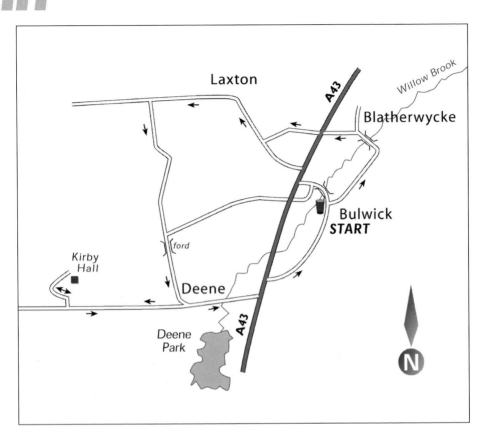

Just over a mile from Laxton, **turn L** (Deene). Follow this quiet lane, ignoring the turn to Bulwick. There is a ford shortly after this turn, but there is rarely any water in it. If there is, take care. After climbing a hill, a **R turn** leads to Kirby Hall. Follow this road until the Hall is signposted down a track to the right. To return to Deene, retrace your route up the track, **turn L** (no signpost) at the road, and **turn R** (Deene) to enter Deene. If you do not want to go to Kirby Hall, do not follow the signs, but keep straight on to Deene.

The wall of Deene Park is now obvious. Follow the road that runs alongside,

through the tiny village. The entrance to Deene Park is off to the right. Carry on along the road to the A43. **Turn L** (Thrapston/Bulwick). Very shortly, **turn R** (Bulwick/King's Cliffe). Follow this road back to Bulwick.

. . . .

DEENE PARK

The Brudenell family have lived at Deene since 1514. In the 16th century the Brudenells were one of the county's small number of influential Catholic families and, like the Treshams and many other Catholic families at the time, they suffered persecution. But the Brudenells later conformed to the Church of England and prospered, whereas the Tresham

Bulwick where the ride starts

fortunes collapsed after the involvement of Francis Tresham in the Gunpowder Plot. The Brudenells eventually became the Earls of Cardigan, with the 7th Earl gaining fame for leading the Charge of the Light Brigade where he showed great bravery and returned from the war a national hero. The house dates mainly from the Tudor period, but was considerably enlarged after 1800, the 7th Earl, notably, adding a ballroom. The house has a touch of the medieval about it, with battlements and a gatehouse. It is open to the public (telephone 01780 450278 or visit www.deenepark.com).

KIRBY HALL

That this magnificent 16th-century house and garden can be enjoyed today is largely down to the restoration carried out by English Heritage. Building of Kirby Hall was started by Humphrey Stafford in 1570. It was then bought, unfinished, by Sir Christopher Hatton. He hoped to impress Queen Elizabeth, to whom he was a dedicated courtier. After 1700 it was used less and less: in the 19th century it decayed. Thus, with restoration, it is a gem from the Renaissance, untouched by Victorian 'improvers'. If you like stately homes, but

The pretty village of Laxton

find most too cluttered with collections, this is for you. Generally it is open daily in July and August and Thursday to Monday the rest of the year (telephone: 0870 333 1181 (general enquiries) or 01536 203230 (Kirby Hall), or visit www.english-heritage.org.uk). There are often special events such as games, tournaments, cookery and dancing, and refreshments can be obtained from reception.

2

Rockingham Castle and the Welland

18½ miles

The broad, steep-sided valley of the Welland, with its many spurs and small villages, has panoramic views. The Welland viaduct is one of the most impressive railway structures in the country and there is historical interest at Lyddington Bede House and Rockingham Castle. Although jet aircraft sometimes use the area around Eyebrook Reservoir for training, there is tranquillity along our route which runs close to the water. One of the great things about this type of route is that it is easily extended or shortened. So you can make as much of a day of it as you please.

Map: OS Landranger 141 Kettering and Corby (GR 907954)

Starting point: There is a small roadside parking space by the picnic tables on the minor road from Gretton to Harringworth, and there is ample parking where the road from Stoke Dry reaches the Eyebrook Reservoir. You may well be able to find parking in other places, but please take care not to block gateways. Although passenger railway lines run nearby, there is no convenient station for this route.

Refreshments: The White Hart, at Lyddington (01572 821703), is well situated and, like the Sun at Great Easton (01536 770273), is a good place to stop. The Sondes Arms, at Rockingham (01536 770312), is just off the route on the way to the castle. The White Swan, at Harringworth (01572 747543), is ideally situated if you started the ride at Eyebrook Reservoir.

The route: Cycling along valley-sides is rarely flat, and this route starts with a long descent, then crosses the valley and eventually heads to the Eyebrook Reservoir, via a sometimes steep climb. The valley is re-crossed. Cottingham and Gretton have short climbs, and if you want to visit Rockingham Castle, this is also at the top of a hill. In all likelihood the downhill sections won't seem as long even though they are longer. The route could easily be extended at either end. Keep straight on at Harringworth to reach Wakerley, where a left turn goes to Barrowden. Keep left at all the junctions in Barrowden and the B672 will take you back to the main route. Equally, carrying on past the Bringhurst turn will eventually take you to Medbourne. There, turn left onto the B664, followed by two more left turns, and then take the road through Ashley and on to Cottingham.

This route can be shortened by taking the minor road from Gretton, crossing the River Welland, and on to the B672.

For the main route, with your back to the valley, **turn L** and soon freewheel under the Welland viaduct and into

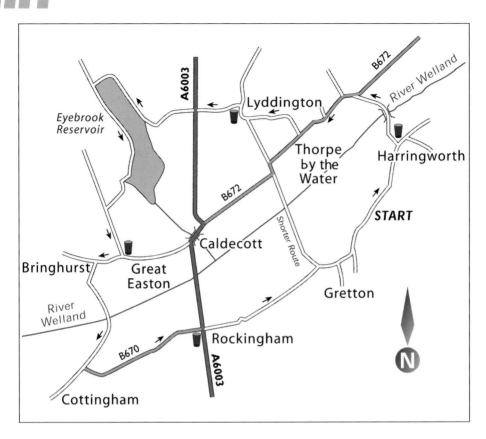

Harringworth. **Turn L**
(Uppingham/Seaton) at the White
Swan. Soon cross the River Welland,
dominated by the viaduct, and enter
Rutland. Go under the viaduct and
keep on this road as it becomes the
B672 (Caldecott). Ignore right turns for
Seaton. Having passed Thorpe by the
Water, **turn R** (no signpost).
*(Continuing straight on to Caldecott,
turning left on the A6003 and, after
leaving the village, right to Great Easton,
will avoid the hills around Lyddington
and Eyebrook Reservoir.)*

There are good views all around. Soon
enter Lyddington. **Turn R** (no
signpost). This is another attractive

village, with a former palace of the
Bishop of Lincoln next to the church.
Further on is a pleasant green with the
stump of the old market cross opposite
the White Hart.

Turn L (Stoke Dry), into Stoke Road.
This road climbs steeply for a short
section. Use it as an excuse to stop and
admire the view back over the village.
At the crossroads with the A6003, go
straight on (Stoke Dry). Descend
through the village to Eyebrook
Reservoir. Follow the road over a bridge
to enter Leicestershire and reach a T-
junction. **Turn L** (Great Easton) and
continue the pleasant ride along the
waterside. After a short climb away

Rockingham, with its castle dominating the village

from the reservoir, reach a T-junction and **turn L** (Great Easton). At the war memorial, near the Sun in Great Easton, **turn R** (Bringhurst/ Medbourne). After passing the primary school, **turn L** (Bringhurst/Cottingham). Pass through Bringhurst, re-cross the Welland and re-enter Northamptonshire before reaching Cottingham.

At the T-junction, **turn L** (Rockingham/Corby). (Superstitious cyclists will not be surprised that the short but memorable climb through Cottingham marks the thirteenth mile of the route.) Leave the village and soon wonderful views emerge on your left. A long freewheel takes you most of the way to a crossroads at the north end of Rockingham village. You will have seen the castle up on the hillside already. Carry straight on at the crossroads (Gretton). Close to Gretton the road climbs once more. There is a pleasant green opposite the church near the top of the hill, but you may well not need a rest just now since carrying straight on will take you back to the starting point within a mile.

The route passes beneath the imposing Welland viaduct

LYDDINGTON BEDE HOUSE

Lyddington was once an important settlement on a main road. The stump of the old market cross can be seen on the village green. It was here that the Bishops of Lincoln turned an old manor house into a palace in the second quarter of the 14th century. Passing to the powerful Cecil family in the 16th century, part of the palace was converted into an almshouse or Bede House for the poor. Inmates were expected to attend church and learn a trade or craft. Attractively situated next to the church, with colourful gardens and shady trees, it is in the care of English Heritage (telephone 01572 822438 or visit www.english-heritage.org.uk).

HARRINGWORTH VIADUCT

Three-quarters of a mile long, with 82 arches, this piece of Victorian civil engineering was opened to traffic in 1879. It dominates the River Welland and the surrounding meadows. Reputed to have 20 million bricks put in place by some 2,500 workmen, it was used mainly by goods trains.

ROCKINGHAM CASTLE

Spectacularly situated amidst the woodland high on the crest of the valleyside and dominating a pretty village, Rockingham Castle cannot be missed, whether one visits it or not. Medieval at heart with major modifications throughout the ages, the

Lyddington

castle was given by Henry VII to the Watson family. It is still owned by them. The grounds contain rare trees and shrubs as well as, according to one legend, King John's treasure. A frequent hunter in Rockingham Forest, John is supposed to have left his treasure chest here shortly before his death. This challenges the tradition that he lost the treasure crossing the Wash. In truth, he was probably pretty well broke at this point in his reign (and anyway digging up the flowerbeds is forbidden!). The castle saw two sieges in the Civil War, the Roundheads successfully capturing the castle and then defending it. Rockingham Castle is open to the public (telephone 01536 770240 or visit www.rockinghamcastle.com).

3

King's Cliffe, Nassington and Fotheringhay

13 miles or 22½ miles

This is a ride of stories. Wansford is sometimes known as Wansford in England because a fenlander, asleep on a hayrick, was washed down the river to this place and told the locals that he came from Long Sutton, in Holland, only to be informed that he was now in Wansford, in England. At Fotheringhay, Mary, Queen of Scots was imprisoned and executed. In the church rests Mary of Valence, Countess of Pembroke, who was married and widowed by an accident in a tournament on the same day. Edward IV, Richard III and

---

Maps: OS Landranger 141 Kettering and Corby and 142 Peterborough (GR 041881)

Starting point: Start in the centre of Oundle, which is easily accessible from the A605 between Peterborough and Thrapston, or via the A427 from Corby. The best parking is at Barnwell Country Park, signposted from the A605 just south of Oundle. From there turn left out of the car park, cross the bridge and follow the road as it bears right signposted Town Centre to get to the war memorial. There is another car park on the A427, just to the west of the town centre, next to the drill hall. A third, long stay, car park is situated off Ashton Road, next to the Jean Strong Centre (GR 044882). This is signed from the A427 to the east of the town centre. There are no railway stations close by but, If you need to arrive by train, Peterborough station is some 9 miles from Wansford, and Stamford station is about 8 miles from King's Cliffe.

Refreshments: There are plenty on this route. In Oundle, the Coffee Tavern in the Market Place and Beans at the main junction are recommended. There is also the Black Horse at Nassington, the Cross Keys at the junction in King's Cliffe, and the King's Head in Apethorpe. (See route 5 for details.)

The route: Passing a range of impressive buildings, the busy centre of Oundle is left behind and lanes lead through an historic landscape to Wansford. There are gentle ups along the valley side, each with a down to compensate. Passing through Forest Enterprise woodland to King's Cliffe, the route then turns south-east along the Willow Brook to Apethorpe and Woodnewton, before turning south to return to Oundle through little Southwick and Glapthorn. There are a few small hills here, but nothing too taxing. Outside of Oundle there is likely to be little traffic and the route is entirely on minor roads.

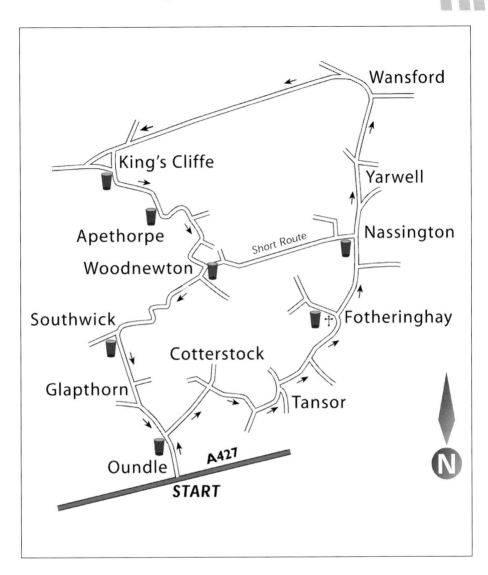

Catherine of Aragon were all associated with the village. At Nassington the scallop shell badge of a medieval pilgrim, priest of that village, can be seen: and there is the Prebendal Manor, some of it dating from the 13th century. King's Cliffe was the home of William Law, who wrote and lent religious books, founded a school for girls and influenced some of the 18th century's most famous people. There, too, are the almshouses set up by Catherine Cornforth who, destitute at the age of eleven, walked to Birmingham to find work. Not to mention the punishment given to the last man sentenced to be whipped in Apethorpe. And for the cyclist, there are few hills and miles of quiet road.

The spectacular church at Fotheringhay

Start at the war memorial in the centre of Oundle at the main junction. Head up the hill (Glapthorn/Southwick). At the George public house, **turn R** (Cotterstock/Woodnewton). At the next crossroads **turn R** (Cotterstock) and immediately enter the village. Pass through it and cross the river. **Turn L** (Fotheringhay/Tansor). Follow this road to Fotheringhay.

Opposite the church in Fotheringhay, **turn R** (Nassington/Yarwell). Follow this road straight through Nassington and Yarwell.

From Nassington, the route can be shortened by turning left (Woodnewton/Apethorpe) at the Black Horse, then turning left (Woodnewton) a little after the church. Pick up the main route at Woodnewton by following signs for Oundle and Fotheringhay.

To continue, keep on to Wansford, **turn L** (King's Cliffe) at the T-junction. *(To go to the centre of Wansford turn right and turn right again at this T-junction and cross the old bridge. Wansford has pubs and shops.)*

On the main route (having turned left), **turn L** again (King's Cliffe). Follow this road until a T-junction is reached. **Turn L** (King's Cliffe/Apethorpe) and pass under an old railway bridge to enter King's Cliffe. At the crossroads near the church, next to the Cross Keys public house, **turn L** (Apethorpe/Fotheringhay/Oundle). Follow this road through Apethorpe (with its village punishment set displayed opposite the church) and Woodnewton (Fotheringhay/Oundle).

After crossing a small bridge, having left Woodnewton, **turn R** (Southwick). Pass through typical Rockingham Forest scenery. In Southwick take the second **turn L** (Glapthorn/Oundle). If you pass the Shuckburgh Arms you have gone too far. Follow this road back to the centre of Oundle.

* *

FOTHERINGHAY

Famous for its castle and the spectacular church, Fotheringhay is delightfully situated amongst the meadows of the Nene valley. There was a castle here before Edmund of Langley, fifth son of Edward III, built the structure that saw the execution of Mary, Queen of Scots. Edmund's grandson, Richard, Duke of York, was buried here by his son, the future Edward IV. Richard had been killed at the Battle of Wakefield, during the Wars of the Roses, his head cut off and placed over Micklegate Bar, in York. Edward retrieved the head, reunited it with the body and brought it to Fotheringhay for burial. He also brought the body of his youngest brother, who had been murdered, and buried it in the same grave. Another brother, Richard III – supposed murderer of the Princes in the Tower – was born at Fotheringhay. It is due to its association with such a wealthy family that the church owes its splendour. The most famous resident of Fotheringhay was, without doubt, Mary, Queen of Scots. She had been Queen of Scotland when a week old, and a widow of the King of France at eighteen. It is said that the thistles on the earthworks – the only remains of the castle – come from seeds scattered by Mary, during her imprisonment. In the 19th century, a ring was found here. It had Mary's initials entwined with those

The lovely town centre of Oundle

of her second husband, Lord Darnley.

The castle site, with the few remains, can be found up a footpath. The motte makes a fine place to view the village and river.

NASSINGTON PREBENDAL MANOR

A prebend was a priest who 'belonged' to a cathedral, but did not live there. Henry I granted several manors around Nassington to Lincoln Cathedral in the early 12th century. The manor provided a residence for the prebend. This charming collection of buildings, close to the church, range in date from the 13th to the 18th centuries. At the time of writing, the house and gardens are open to the public on bank holiday Mondays and every Wednesday and Sunday from Easter to the end of September. Refreshments are available and there are numerous special events (telephone 01780 782575, or visit www.prebendal-manor.demon.co.uk).

4

Around Barnwell and Warmington

12 miles or 15 miles

Cycling through these little country lanes along the placid valley of the Nene – with even more placid bovines grazing by the riverside – and through broad acres of ripening wheat, it is easy to imagine that nothing much has happened here. But it has – and does. Ashton is the home of the World Conker Championships, attracting an international field, and Barnwell has a castle, though you will be lucky to get more than a glimpse of it as it is only rarely open to the public. The merits of this ride are quiet roads and picturesque villages.

Maps: Barnwell is just on OS Landranger 141 Kettering and Corby, but all bar a couple of miles of the route are on 142 Peterborough (GR 055883)

Starting point: Start at the village green facing the church. There is no designated car parking on this route. There is plenty of space in Ashton, but please show consideration when parking. If you wish to start at Warmington, you will have to take the off-road option between there and Ashton. There is no railway station really convenient for this route.

Refreshments: The Chequered Skipper at Ashton (01832 273494) will provide good beer and fine food. Moreover, the extensive green surrounded by trees makes this the perfect spot for a refreshing drink on a sunny day. The Montagu Arms, in Barnwell (01832 273726), is everything a country pub should be in such a lovely spot. There is a shop near the church in Warmington.

The route: From Ashton the ride goes to the east of the Nene Valley, with some pleasant views, before passing through Barnwell. The roads become increasingly minor on the way to Lutton via Hemington, and are scarcely busier on the way to Warmington. From Warmington to Ashton, the direct route involves two stretches of byway: one rough and stony, one rough and potentially muddy after heavy rain. Both are easily cycled. There is also a small rifle range to be passed through, so do watch for any red flags and follow instructions. This belongs to Oundle School and is only a few yards wide. However, if you don't wish to cycle through the range, or indeed if rain has made the route too wet, then follow the slightly shorter alternative after Lutton.

In Ashton, face the church and head left, out of the village. Before long arrive at a T-junction. **Turn L** (no signpost). Go up the gentle slope and **turn R** (Barnwell/Armston). Keep on this road to Barnwell. The peaceful meadows by the river, with Armston set back on a wooded hillside, make for

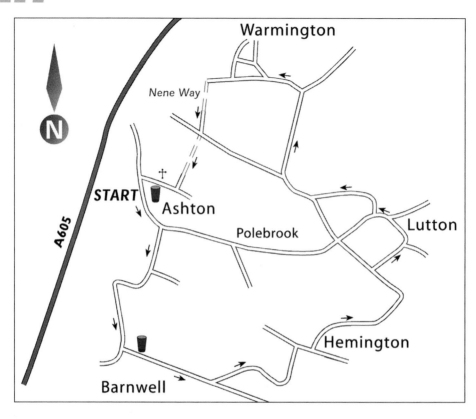

timeless views. Keep straight on for Barnwell. As you enter Barnwell you can get a glimpse of the castle through a gateway on the left. Shortly after this, **turn L** (Thurning and Hemington) into Church Hill. There is a village shop here and at the bottom of the hill on the village green is the Montagu Arms.

Leave Barnwell by keeping straight ahead on Hemington Road. Where the road forks, keep left for Hemington and Luddington. At the T-junction **turn R** (Luddington/Great Gidding/Lutton) and immediately enter Hemington. In Hemington **turn L** (Lutton). Follow the road past Hemington House, bearing sharp left. **Turn R** (Lutton).

In Lutton, **turn L** (Polebrook/Oundle).

Now you need to decide whether to go to Warmington and follow the rough byways to Ashton, or to stick to tarmac roads. If you decide to miss out Warmington, pass through Lutton, following the road as it bends left on leaving the village. After a mile or so, go straight on at the crossroads for Polebrook. In Polebrook keep right and then take the right turn for Ashton, returning to the green by the road on which you left.

To continue on to Warmington, **turn R** (Papley) where the main road bears left on the edge of the village. Follow this as it turns sharp left at the sign for Papley Farm Cottages. At the T-

Ashton where this rides begins

junction, **turn R** (Warmington), then, at the end of the wood, **turn R** (no signpost). There are broad views to the left. At the T-junction **turn L**, (Warmington/Elton) and descend with Warmington clearly in front of you.

On the edge of Warmington, **turn L** into Taylor's Green. If you want to go into the village you can get back to Taylor's Green by turning left, a little way after the church and village hall, into Spinney Close. **Turn R** at the end to regain the main route.

Just before reaching the farmyard, **turn L** on a byway, which is rough for

a short way. This is signed as the Nene Valley Way. Shortly after passing some barns on your left, this becomes a properly surfaced road. At the crossroads, go straight on along another rough track, which soon improves again. This is shown on the map as the Roman road from Thrapston to Durobrivae, near Peterborough, though it winds around enough to make you doubt it.

Pass the rifle range and return to tarmac. At the T-junction, **turn R** (Nene Way) soon reaching the thatched houses and tree-girt green of Ashton. The Chequered Skipper is on the left.

The River Nene flows peacefully near Armston

BARNWELL

Barnwell Castle and gardens are private and are open to the public only on rare occasions. The castle became the property of the Montagu family during the Tudor period and was used as an arsenal by the Royalists in the Civil War: an uncomfortable position between staunchly Roundhead Northampton and Oliver Cromwell's home county. Twenty-nine Montagus are buried in the church, opposite which are some almshouses built by Nicholas Latham – rector of the parish. He also paid for the building of almshouses in Oundle and five free schools in the area.

ASHTON AND THE WORLD CONKER CHAMPIONSHIPS

Each October, this quiet village plays host to the World Conker Championships, generally on the second Sunday of the month. What could be better than a brisk ride on an autumn morning, followed by a pint or two over a day of international sporting competition on the village green? The whole affair aims to raise money for charitable purposes. Visit www.worldconkerchampionships.com where you can find out all you might need to know – and a good deal more.

5

Oundle to Boughton

24 miles or 29 miles

The busy market town of Oundle makes a good start for a ride. All the necessary facilities are there and it is an attractive place to wile away some time. The many fine stone buildings, from the 16th century onward, which make it such a delightful spot include the almshouses, inns, town hall, public school and private houses. Moreover, they are set amongst gentle pastoral countryside, with the River Nene on three sides, and a graceful church spire that rises above the steeply-pitched roofs and dormer windows. A few miles away,

---

Maps: OS Landranger 141 Kettering and Corby (GR 041881)

Starting point: Oundle is the logical place to start this route. It is easily accessible from the A605 between Peterborough and Thrapston, or via the A427 from Corby. Follow signs for parking. The nearest railway station to the route is at Kettering on the line from London to Leicester. Follow signs from the town centre for the A4300 towards Weekley, turning off for Warkton to join the route at Grafton Underwood. This is a distance of some 6 miles. An equally good starting place, with car park, toilets and information, would be the Fermyn Woods Country Park on the A6116 near Brigstock. It lacks the facilities of Oundle, but refreshments can be obtained in Brigstock village.

Refreshments: In Oundle, the Coffee Tavern (01832 272524) in the Market Place and Beans (01832 270007) at the main junction are recommended, though there are plenty of alternative choices. The Woolpack (01832 733118) and the Rose and Crown (01832 272339), both in Islip, are a little over halfway round. The Shuckburgh Arms, at Stoke Doyle (01832 272339), is particularly convenient if you have followed the by-way.

The route: The first 2 miles out of Oundle are on the A427. This is generally not too busy, but can carry significant traffic at peak hours. However, the cars soon thin out before the turn is made to Lyveden New Bield and eventually to Brigstock. Just before Brigstock the route uses a short section of the A6116, another generally quiet main road. The terrain undulates to Grafton Underwood. Here there is an option to go to Geddington via Boughton House. This 'there-and-back' diversion adds about 5 miles to the journey. Minor roads continue to Slipton and a mixture of old main road and cycle track carries the route past Islip and back onto minor roads along the gentle Nene Valley. This is not an easy route to cut short, there are byways and bridleways, some of which could be followed, but few of which match up. The best shortcut, in my view, is described in the text.

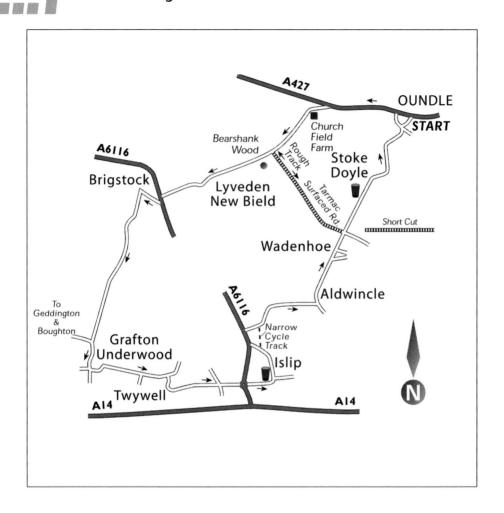

Lyveden New Bield stands alone, unfinished, a testimony to an ambitious builder of remarkable faith. The countryside rolls on to Brigstock and Grafton Underwood, a village of stone and thatch, with a stream running by the road. From here, a detour will take those interested and with energy to Boughton House, the 'Versailles of the North', once home to a man who wanted to plant an avenue of trees all the way to London. No less ambitious was King Edward I, builder of the Eleanor Cross at Geddington, a mile further on. At Twywell, the journals of the 19th-century explorer and missionary David Livingstone were prepared for publication. One wonders what the two Africans, who brought Livingstone's body back to Britain and stayed in the village to help with the detail of the journals, made of life here. After this the route drops to the Nene Valley at Islip, turns north and follows it through peaceful pastures and quiet villages back to Oundle.

A short diversion will take you to Geddington

Start at the main junction by the war memorial in the centre of Oundle, and looking towards the Talbot Hotel head left, along West Street. This is the A427. Just before the church, **turn R** (Lyveden New Bield/Benefield) into a one-way street. Very shortly, at a T-junction, **turn R** (Benefield). A couple of miles from the start, **turn L** (Churchfield/Lyveden New Bield). This road is followed almost all the way to Brigstock, passing the track that leads to Lyveden New Bield, clearly visible on the left, near Lyveden Old Bield.

It is possible to cut the route short about a mile after Churchfield and a mile short of Lyveden Old Bield. A byway turns left off the road towards a wood on a low hill. It does not look promising unless you are into off-road cycling. However, where it reaches the wood at the crest of the hill, it becomes a rough, rutted track, and shortly after a properly surfaced lane. This rejoins the main route near Wadenhoe.

On reaching the A6116, **turn L** (Thrapston/Brigstock). Very shortly the entrance to Fermyn Woods Country Park is reached. This would make a good alternative starting point, with car park, toilets and information. Shortly, **turn R** (Brigstock). Brigstock has an interesting village centre, but the route **turns L** (Grafton/Cranford) before reaching it. Follow this road up and down before flattening out to enter the pretty estate village of Grafton Underwood.

If you want to do a 'there-and-back' diversion to Boughton House or

In the village of Stoke Doyle

Geddington, **turn R** (Geddington/Boughton House). The road passes the entrance to Boughton House and soon after enters Geddington and reaches the Eleanor Cross, with the old bridge to the left. Retrace the route to get back to Grafton Underwood. This diversion amounts to a total of 5 miles: downhill there, uphill back. **Turn R** (Slipton and Cranford) at the T-junction to regain the main route.

Pass through Grafton Underwood, then, at the crossroads, **turn L** (Slipton/Thrapston). After 1½ miles, **turn R** (Twywell/Woodford). Follow this road through Twywell, passing the Old Friar pub, eventually running parallel to the A14, to a roundabout. Continue straight on (Islip). Descend to the village and **turn L** (Islip) by the Woolpack public house, into Chapel Hill. Pass the magnificent gates to the play area, continuing on this road. As the main road is approached, pick up the cycle track on the right, which cuts out a short stretch of main road.

Turn R (Aldwincle/Wadenhoe). In Aldwincle, at the T-junction, **turn L** (Stoke Doyle/Oundle). There is a shop in Aldwincle. Follow this road all the way to Oundle. At the T-junction, **turn R** (no signpost) and, very shortly, **turn L** (Town Centre), to return to the market place.

● ●

LYVEDEN NEW BIELD
Thomas Tresham was born at the Old Bield, but his ambitious plans for the New

Bield were swept away by his death. The gardens and garden lodge remain as a 400-year-old time-capsule, and a testament to his piety. They are now in the care of the National Trust, with the garden and orchard undergoing restoration. The lonely isolation adds to a slightly melancholy atmosphere created by the unfulfilled magnificence. Other Tresham buildings nearby are the unusual Market House at Rothwell and the mysteriously symbolic Triangular Lodge at Rushton. Rushton Hall was the Tresham family home. Lyveden New Bield is open to the public. (Telephone 01832 205358 or visit www.nationaltrust.org.uk.)

BOUGHTON HOUSE
One of the great houses of Europe, the home of the Duke of Buccleuch and Queensberry, has been in the same family for 450 years. The estate is the hub of the Living Landscape Trust, and various parts of the house and grounds are open to the public, but, since the house is open to the public for limited periods only, it is wise to check first (telephone 01536 515731 or visit www.boughtonhouse.org.uk). Combining an afternoon at Boughton House with the entire ride would make for a long day, with 14 miles still to go to complete the ride. However, for those so inclined there are art treasures, gardens and an armoury. There is a real attempt to show how a great estate impacted on the landscape, culture and economy of the locality and the nation.

ELEANOR CROSSES
Edward I was prosecuting his ambitious claims to be overlord of Scotland when he heard of the death of his Queen, Eleanor of Castile. She was on her way

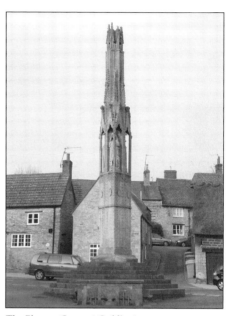

The Eleanor Cross at Geddington

north to join Edward, but died on the journey at Harby, in Nottinghamshire. Edward arranged for an elaborate monument to be erected at each place where the funeral cortege halted on the two-week journey back to London. The crosses at Geddington and Hardingstone, in Northamptonshire, are still to be seen. The slender cross at Geddington is set amongst old stone buildings in the junction of three roads. In 1290 the coffin may have rested in the hunting lodge that monarchs had used for many years. In an age when marriages of monarchs were often political contracts, Edward and Eleanor are said genuinely to have loved one another. The crosses were just one mark of this. Edward also ordered that two candles should burn constantly at her tomb: they did so until the 16th century.

6

Higham Ferrers and the Nene Valley

12 miles, 24 miles or 29 miles

Between Wellingborough and Thrapston, the River Nene (pronounced *nenn* between source and Thrapston and *neen* thereafter) flows through a broad valley, past numerous small towns and villages. To help the miles go by, you could see who can count the most church spires in view. Higham Ferrers has been a borough since 1251. Now bypassed, it is still a busy town, with a spectacular parish church, the remains of a college founded by a son of a Higham merchant who became Archbishop of Canterbury, and many other attractive buildings. You could add a few miles by taking in the Bedfordshire villages of Yelden, with well-

Maps: OS Landranger 153 Bedford and Huntingdon and 141 Kettering and Corby. Higham Ferrers is on 153 (GR 961685)

Starting point: For convenience, the starting point is at the car park in the market square. However, more useful parking is signposted off the High Street. Market Place car parking has time restrictions which make it unlikely to be of use to all but the very swiftest of riders or those doing the route on a Sunday. Thrapston would also make a good starting point. You could use the parking at the pocket park by the old gravel workings on the Addington road out of Ringstead. If you do, note that there is a height limit at the entrance. The nearest station to Higham Ferrers is at Wellingborough, some 6 miles away, along quite busy roads.

Refreshments: The Green Dragon, Higham Ferrers (01933 312088), opposite Chichele College, is convenient for the start. The Tasty Bite Victorian Tea Shoppe, Thrapston (01832 733070), is a short way off-route to the right. The Hare and Hounds, Great Addington (01536 330661), has a garden and serves food. There are picnic spots by the river at Denford or on the green at Woodford.

The route: Shortly after leaving Higham Ferrers there is a choice – a longer route into Bedfordshire on country lanes or 5 miles on the B645 (which is not busy under normal circumstances). The hills are gentle on both. The routes meet between Hargrave and Raunds. Raunds is the obvious place to shorten the distance as the route skirts both sides of this small town. After Raunds the main route follows a narrow lane before picking up on the ghost of the A605 alongside the Raunds to Thrapston road. From Thrapston the route follows minor roads, up and down hill, to re-cross the valley. The busy A605 roundabout at Raunds is where most traffic will be encountered: from there a mixture of B roads and minor roads forms the last section of the route.

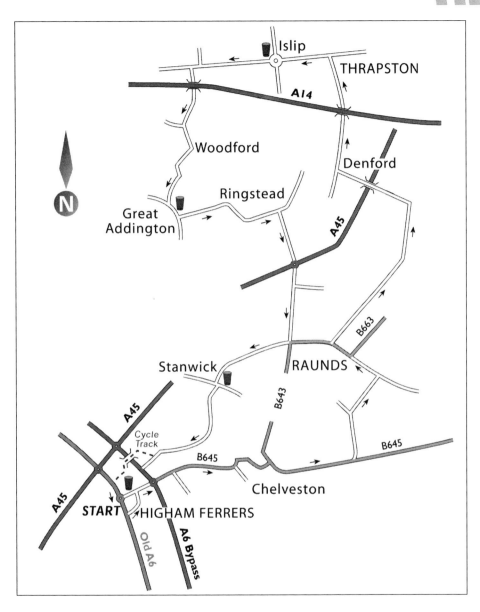

preserved earthworks of a motte and bailey castle, Upper Dean and Shelton. The main route is rejoined after 'idyllic' Hargrave, before passing on to Raunds. From there the route dips down to the riverside at Denford. The Nene is crossed on the old bridge between Thrapston and Islip, before undulating through Woodford, with its large greens, and Great Addington. A return is made through Ringstead to Raunds, to follow quiet roads back to Higham Ferrers.

Islip from the Thrapston bridge

From the small car park in the Market Square, **turn L** onto the main road and straight away **turn L** (no signpost) into Market Square, which soon becomes Wood Street and then Midland Road, follow it round to the left. At the crossroads, **turn R** (no signpost). After turning you will see a signpost for a major roundabout ahead. At the roundabout, go straight over (St Neots/Kimbolton). This is the B645. (*To avoid the 5 miles of this road and for a longer ride, see the last paragraph of directions.*) For the main route, follow it through Chelveston. A couple of miles beyond Chelveston, **turn L** (no signpost) onto a weight restricted road. This is the first proper road on the left after Chelveston. Soon pass New England Farm. A little further on, where the road bears left, **turn R**

(Hargrave). At the T-junction, **turn L** (Raunds/Keyston).

The extension through Yelden rejoins the main route here.

Follow this lane to the B663 and **turn L** (Raunds). Descend towards Raunds. Where the road bears left to the centre of Raunds, **turn R** (Denford/Thrapston). *Keeping left will enable you to cut the overall distance in half by passing through the centre of Raunds to pick up signs for Stanwick.* For the main route, follow the lane as it veers sharply to the left, crosses over the A45 by a bridge and starts to descend to the Nene Valley. At the T-junction, **turn R** (Denford/Thrapston). Follow this road through Denford, past the Cock, and reach the riverside. Pass under the A14 into Thrapston. At the mini-roundabout, the town centre is to the right. For the main route **turn L** (no signpost) and soon pass the Bridge Hotel.

Cross over the bridge into Islip. Carry straight on, with the Woolpack Inn on your right. Follow this road over a roundabout (Twywell/Woodford). Pass a small industrial area and **turn L** (Woodford/The Addingtons). Pass under the A14 and through Woodford. Having probably gone up and down the gears, arrive in Great Addington. **Turn L** (Raunds/Ringstead) immediately after the Hare and Hounds pub. This road crosses the River Nene and soon bears left, past old gravel workings, now a pocket park, to reach Ringstead.

At the crossroads, next to the New Inn, **turn R** (Raunds/Stanwick). Climb steadily to a roundabout on the A45. This road can be busy. Cross straight over (Raunds/Chelveston), with care. At the next roundabout go straight on again (Raunds/Chelveston). Follow this road to a third roundabout next to the Red Lion. **Turn R** (Stanwick/Higham Ferrers). In Stanwick, immediately after the church, **turn L** and immediately **R** (no signpost), just before the post office. If you pass the Duke of Wellington you have gone too far! Ignore the sign to Higham that takes you onto the main road.

Follow this road as it winds gently upward out of the village. Soon you will see Higham Ferrers church in the distance. Eventually the A6 dual

The River Nene at Denford

carriageway is reached. Use the bridge to the right to rejoin the route on the other side of the A6. Pass through some bollards and keep straight on and enter Higham Ferrers. **Turn L** (no signpost) at the T-junction. Follow this road straight on at a roundabout to return to the Market Square.

The main route uses the B645 for 5 miles. If you want to avoid this road, which is not usually busy, using minor roads instead, it can be done by adding an extra 5 miles to the overall distance to make a total of 29 miles. *Directions for this alternative:* after crossing the A6 roundabout outside Higham Ferrers onto the B645, **turn R** (Newton Bromswold); at the T-junction **turn R** (Newton Bromswold); at the top of a short hill where the road bears sharp right, **turn L** (Yelden) (effectively straight on) and very shortly **turn L** (Yelden) again; follow this road through Yelden; a mile and a half after Yelden, **turn L** (Upper Dean); in Upper Dean **turn L** (Shelton) before reaching the church; follow the road through Shelton to bear sharply to the left; at the B645 **turn L** (Chelveston) and shortly **turn R** (Raunds) to rejoin the main route a mile after leaving Hargrave.

HIGHAM FERRERS

Now bypassed by the A6 and a neighbour to much larger Rushden, Higham was important before 1066. It already had the right to hold a market at the time of Domesday Book and may even have had defensive walls built by the Saxons. It certainly had a castle near the church, but nothing of it now remains. The parish church is thought by many to be one of the most magnificent in the county. The spire is spectacular and there are impressive carvings and brasses. Close to it is a school (which was a chantry before Henry VIII abolished it) and a bede house – a sort of almshouse. About 150 yards away are the peaceful remains of a college – home to clerics who lived rather like monks but without the strict rules. The magnificence of the church owes a good deal to the patronage of the Earls of Derby and of Lancaster, but mostly to Henry Chichele, Archbishop of Canterbury, from 1414 to 1443. Son of a merchant of the borough, Henry founded St John's College and All Souls' College, Oxford, but never forgot Higham. He contributed to the church, built the college, the bede house and the school. The old buildings of the town centre are surrounded by developments from the age of the boot and shoe industry and modern housing estates.

INDUSTRY IN THE NENE VALLEY

In the Middle Ages, the wealth created through agriculture paid for the many church spires to be seen, and wealthy landowners paid for wall-paintings such as the ones in Raunds' church. Later, as the leather industries developed, Raunds and the surrounding villages were at the eastern end of the 'boot and shoe belt'. By the end of the 19th century conditions for the workers in the shoemaking trade were in a poor state, eventually declining to such an extent that some workers from 'Red' Raunds marched on London – one completing the journey on crutches – to appeal to the government for relief. There was also some iron quarrying and iron production around Islip and Twywell, while even little towns such as Thrapston had small engineering works. Today, light industry and logistics are significant occupations in the area, and the proximity of major roads and motorways make Northamptonshire an ideal location.

7

Around Arthingworth

13½ miles

Crossing the River Jordan comes as a surprise to most visitors to this area, though were it not for the sign, few, if any, would be aware of it. The River Jordan here is neither deep nor wide and Michael would be hard pushed to sail a paper yacht on it. Still, it runs through the pretty village of Braybrooke, one of three, together with Arthingworth and Harrington, visited on this route. There are many fine views over the mixed farming land through which the lanes wind, rise and fall. This is the sort of country that the huntsmen of the Midlands used to love and one can imagine the thrill of a steeplechase to Desborough, Rothwell or Market Harborough.

Map: OS Landranger 141 Kettering and Corby (GR 746805)

Starting point: The picnic area and car park by the old railway bridge, a little way along the minor road to Arthingworth from the A508. This is about 1 mile north of the A14/A508 junction. Market Harborough station is some 3½ miles from the track to Arthingworth and 5 miles from the start. Signs for Sustrans Route Six (Brampton Valley Way) can be picked up in the town centre. The Oxendon Tunnel, between Market Harborough and the start, requires lights and care.

Refreshments: The Bull's Head, Arthingworth (01858 525637), 'welcomes walkers and cyclists' and serves food; the Swan, Braybrooke (01858 462754) and the Tollemache Arms, Harrington (01536 710469) will also meet the needs of cyclists.

The route: Starting along the Brampton Valley Way towards Market Harborough, then following a former road – now a track – to Arthingworth. The byway to Arthingworth has a solid tarmac surface, though there are some potholes to watch out for. After that, country lanes, some very minor, are the order of the day for the rest of the trip. Flat as far as Arthingworth, there is a rollercoaster to Braybrooke, followed by a short flat section. Then a good climb is followed by a stirring descent and another, gentler ascent. A broad country road passes through Harrington, before a minor road descends (well, mostly) back to the starting point.

Either carry your bike up the steps to the Brampton Valley Way or reach it by following the wheelchair access sign. Whichever you do, head north by turning right.

After 1½ miles or so, where a gate gives access to a tarmac track, **turn R** (Arthingworth) to pass through a second gate a little way ahead. Follow this track all the way to Arthingworth.

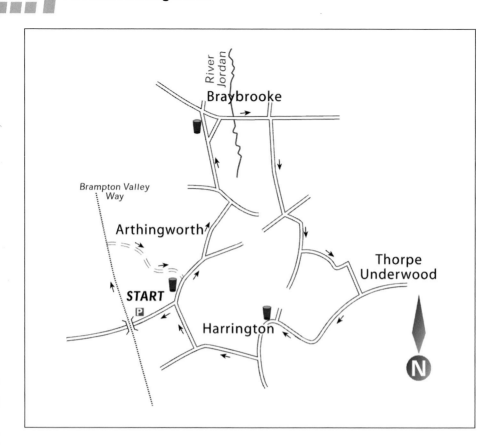

The Bull's Head is just to the right at the T-junction next to the church. **Turn L** (Braybrooke/Desborough). After a cattle grid, **turn L** (Braybrooke). After another cattle grid, at a T-junction, **turn L** (no signpost) and almost immediately **turn R** (Braybrooke). Follow this road, with good views to the left, into the village.

Keep straight ahead past the Swan and reach a crossroads next to the church. **Turn R** (Desborough/Kettering), to cross the River Jordan. After a mile or so, at a crossroads, **turn R** (Thorpe Underwood/Harrington) and climb steadily to another crossroads. *A right turn here would take you down to*

Arthingworth and back to the start – a total distance of some 8 miles. The main route goes straight on (Harrington/Thorpe Underwood). A long descent follows, ending with a sharp bend over a narrow bridge. Immediately after the bridge, **turn L** (Thorpe Underwood). This lovely little lane rises gently through the scattered settlement of Thorpe Underwood, with a mix of woodland and open views.

At a T-junction, **turn R** (Harrington). Pass through Harrington. At the far end of the village, **turn R** (Arthingworth/Kelmarsh). There are good views along this section, especially down to Arthingworth.

Turn **R** (Braybrooke/Arthingworth) and descend to the valley. At the T-junction, **turn L** (Kelmarsh/Northampton/Market Harborough). Before long the old railway bridge next to the car park comes into view.

THE BRAMPTON VALLEY WAY

The former route of the railway line, between Northampton and Market Harborough, now makes an excellent leisure facility for walkers, riders and cyclists. As part of Sustrans Route Six, it forms part of a long-distance cycle route from Oxford to York. There are two tunnels, which provide added entertainment for children of all ages. However, remember that there are other users and that cyclists should give way to horses and walkers. At frequent intervals along the way are benches, artwork and signposts.

BRAYBROOKE

For a short while in the late 14th/early 15th century, Braybrooke was a centre of religious heresy. Sir Thomas Latimer was a Lollard (the name given to the followers of John Wycliffe, and the only extensive heresy in England in the Middle Ages), and was frequently in trouble with the Church authorities. He used his influence to maintain Robert Hook, a Lollard, as village priest. Lollardy seems to have survived amongst some people in the area even after Sir Thomas's death. The Latimer family had a castle and manor in the village, the remains of which are no more than grassy mounds in the field close to the bridge. In the church is the wooden effigy of another Sir Thomas Latimer, Member of Parliament in the late 13th/early 14th century.

The village of Braybrooke – once a centre of religious heresy

8

Naseby and Holdenby

15 miles, 20 miles or 31 miles

The decisive battle of the English Civil War was fought at Naseby in 1645. Later, Charles I was held prisoner at Holdenby Hall. This ride takes you to both places, and much more. Cottesbrooke Hall has justly famous gardens,

---

Map: OS Landranger 141 Kettering and Corby (GR 737707)

Starting point: There is a car park where the Brampton Valley Way is crossed by the minor road between Spratton and Brixworth. It is reached by turning off the A5199 in Spratton, signposted Brixworth, or from the A508 through Brixworth, following signs for Spratton. It could be reached from Northampton station, though this would make a long route 14 miles longer, by following Sustrans Route Six: turn right from the station approach to cross over the railway and pick up the signs. The northern end of the ride can be reached from Market Harborough station, by picking up signs for Sustrans Route Six heading south from the town centre. It is about 4 miles to the route, a mile south of Great Oxendon tunnel: you will need lights!

Refreshments: The Red Lion at East Haddon (01604 770223), which advertises 'gourmet bar food', is recommended, and is in an interesting old building. In Naseby, there is the Fitzgerald Arms (01604 740273), and the Old Red Lion at Clipston (01858 525257) is near the green. There are not many other opportunities for refreshments, especially if the various halls and houses are not open, so it is best to go prepared. Ravensthorpe Reservoir, Creaton and Clipston greens (or any of the benches along the Brampton Valley Way) would make good places to picnic.

The route: Minor roads all the way, except a short stretch of B road. The traffic-free Brampton Valley Way, which forms part of Sustrans Route Six, is used. Do not be put off by the unlit Kelmarsh Tunnel, just ensure that your lights work. The alternative route around the tunnel is longer and may well require some carrying. There are several hills worthy of note, especially between Teeton and Cottesbrooke. In compensation there are exhilarating downhills (but take care). After Cottesbrooke the road rises steadily to Naseby, before flattening out across the battlefield. It then descends to the old railway line near Kelmarsh, after which it is virtually flat. It is a long route, but can be shortened – especially if you want to visit places along the way – by using the little lanes between Cottesbrooke and the start, via a short section of the Brampton Valley Way. Directions are given directly to and from Cottesbrooke from the starting point at the appropriate place in the main route description.

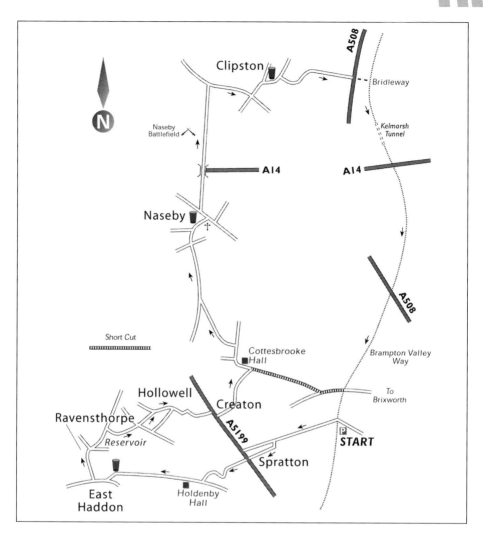

as well as being an interesting Queen Anne period house. Lamport Hall and Kelmarsh Hall also are close by the route. There is a section along the traffic-free Brampton Valley Way – the former railway between Northampton and Market Harborough. This includes a ride through an unlit tunnel. This can feel quite adventurous – children love it – but use lights (both front and rear) and take care. Added to all this and making up for the long flat section along the railway, there are good views from the numerous hills. Ravensthorpe Reservoir and the roads around Cottesbrooke are a joy. For steam railway fans, a couple of miles down the Brampton Valley Way towards Northampton, is the Northampton and Lamport Railway (www.nlr.org.uk or telephone 01604 820327). This long route can easily be shortened, but why not make a day of it and savour the variety.

The village green at Creaton

From the car park **turn L** (Spratton). After the traffic calming chicane **turn L** (no signpost) into Yew Tree Lane. Follow it to the right as it becomes Holdenby Road. At the T-junction **turn L** (no signpost) to carry on along Holdenby Road. Cross the A5199, with care, towards Holdenby. As the road climbs – you may need to get off and push – bear round to the left (Holdenby/East Haddon). At the T-junction, **turn R** (Holdenby/East Haddon). Soon pass the entrance to Holdenby Hall.

At the T-junction, next to the church, in the centre of East Haddon, **turn R** (no signpost). Follow this road as it bears right (Ravensthorpe/Guilsborough). Enjoy the long descent from East Haddon. Then try to enjoy the climb up to Ravensthorpe and follow the road through the village. Descend to Ravensthorpe Reservoir. The reservoir is popular with fishermen and bird watchers. Immediately after crossing the reservoir **turn R** (Hollowell). There is a small car park by the reservoir which would make a good

spot for a picnic (also as an alternative starting point).

The road climbs and reaches a crossroads. Go straight on (Hollowell). At the T-junction, **turn R** (Hollowell). Descend through Hollowell and follow the road to Creaton. At the A5199, **turn R** (Northampton) and very shortly **turn L** (Cottesbrooke). Descend through Creaton and, at the bottom of the hill, **turn L** (Cottesbrooke). Follow the road to Cottesbrooke.

*If you want to return to the start from Cottesbrooke, **turn R** (Brixworth). Follow this road to a T-junction and **turn L** (no signpost). Soon cross over an old railway bridge. Immediately after the bridge, **turn L** (Brampton Valley Way) and descend a narrow track. Then **turn L** (Spratton Road car park/Merry Tom Crossing). Follow the track to return to the start.*

To get directly to Cottesbrooke from the Spratton Road car park, cross the road on leaving the car park and follow the Brampton Valley Way (Creaton

*Road/Houghton Crossing). Immediately after passing under a bridge, **turn R** (Creaton Road). Ascend a narrow track. At the road **turn R** (Cottesbrooke Village) and cross the bridge. Where the road veers left, **turn R** (no signpost) and follow the road to Cottesbrooke. At the T- junction **turn R** (Haselbech/Naseby) to rejoin the main route.*

To do the main route in one go, ignore the right turn for Brixworth in Cottesbrooke. Instead follow the road through the village, passing the church, towards Haselbech and Naseby. On leaving Cottesbrooke, ignore the first left turn signposted Guilsborough. Shortly after passing a farm amongst some trees on the right, **turn L** (no signpost) along a gated road. Follow this quiet lane. At the T-junction **turn R** (no signpost) and in a few yards pass Vale Farm. Follow this road to Naseby.

In Naseby, at a T-junction, **turn R** (Clipston/Battlefield

Obelisk/Monument). Opposite the church, **turn L** (Sibbertoft/Monument). As you start to descend, **turn R** (Sibbertoft/Monument) and soon cross the A14 by a bridge. Follow this road past the monument. At the T-junction, **turn R** (Clipston). Then **turn L** (Clipston) at a crossroads. Opposite the Old Red Lion, **turn R** (Kelmarsh). Go down High Street, passing the beautiful primary school. Keep left at the church as the road becomes Church Lane. Follow this to the A508.

At the A508, an unpromisingly rough track will be seen opposite, barred by a gate. Go straight across the main road and use the small, wooden gate on the left to get to the track. Follow the track to the old railway bridge and **turn R** (Northampton) along the Brampton Valley Way. (After a while you will see signs for the diversionary route to avoid Kelmarsh Tunnel.) Keep to the right and have your lights ready. The surface is fairly good, but be aware of a

Light at the end of Kelmarsh Tunnel

few bumps. At the end of the tunnel go through a wooden gate to pass under the A14 and then through a second wooden gate to regain the old trackbed. Follow this all the way back to Spratton Road car park. The journey is done.

THE BATTLE OF NASEBY

Naseby stands on the watershed of the Midlands: the Avon flows to the west, streams to the Nene to the east. It is also at the watershed of the past. Whether the victory won by the Parliamentarians over the Royalists on 14th June 1645 was one for liberty or started a descent into anarchy is a matter for historians. What is in no doubt is that the cavalry charge led by Oliver Cromwell drove the Royalists from the field decisively. Until then the outcome had been in the balance, despite Parliament's superior numbers. The difference between the sides was really Cromwell's ability to keep discipline amongst his cavalry following their charge. He brought them back to the battle, whilst Prince Rupert was unable to do the same with his cavalry, that had been successful on the other flank. Cromwell's returned; Rupert's set to chasing the enemy and looting. The battlefield lies to the north-west of the village, on the road to Sibbertoft.

HOLDENBY HOUSE, GARDENS AND FALCONRY CENTRE

After his defeat at Naseby, Charles I fell back on Oxford, his base throughout the Civil War. In desperation he secretly went north, to try to make an agreement with the invading Scots army that was besieging Newark. However, they handed him over to the English Parliament and Charles found himself under arrest at Holdenby House, not far from Naseby. The four months he spent there seem not to have been too hard. Until a party of

soldiers arrived to take him into the possession of the army, he had often ridden to Althorp or Boughton to play bowls. He also read poetry, but had to put up with two hours of sermons a day from a cleric sent by Parliament to teach him the error of his ways. Much of the original house was destroyed shortly after. Today, the house and gardens are open to the public, along with a falconry centre. There are often special events. For information, visit www.holdenby.com or call 01604 770074. The falconry centre website is at www.icarusfalconry.co.uk.

COTTESBROOKE HALL AND GARDENS

The village of Cottesbrooke, set in delightful countryside, is reached by quiet lanes, which add to a feeling of isolation. The church and almshouses are picturesque, but visitors are generally drawn by the hall and gardens. The first is a fine Queen Anne (1702-14) building, that replaced an earlier mansion. Some claim that it was the inspiration for Jane Austen's *Mansfield Park*, though it must be said that it is not the only one in the field for that title. For those with an interest in sporting paintings, the Woolavington Collection – one of the best in the world – is housed here. The park was landscaped in the 18th century by an unknown designer. The formal and wild gardens have been developed over the centuries. All can be visited. Telephone 01604 505808 for information, or visit www.cottesbrookehall.co.uk.

Also on this route is Kelmarsh Hall (01604 686543), a mansion house, garden and park, with a herd of British White cattle. The house and grounds are in the care of a preservation trust. It is sometimes open and has special events. Information on 01604 686543.

9
Pitsford Water and Lamport
19 miles

Bright sunshine brings the crowds to Pitsford Water at weekends. The track around the lake is popular with both cyclists and walkers, providing generally flat traffic-free riding. Once away from the lake, gently undulating countryside returns, and quiet lanes make for a peaceful ride. The route goes through the attractive village of Scaldwell before passing close to Lamport Hall, once the home of the Isham family. Near the start, in Brixworth, is an important Saxon church (see notes at end of chapter). The route also passes an old airfield from which secret missions were flown by the USAAF into Nazi-occupied Europe during the Second World War.

Maps: OS Landranger 141 Kettering and Corby. A very short stretch from Walgrave, through Holcot to the car park is on 152 Northampton and Milton Keynes (GR 781701)

Starting point: Brixworth Country Park can be reached by following the signs to Pitsford Water and Holcot from a roundabout on the A508 at the northern end of Brixworth. The car park is on the Brixworth to Holcut road just to the west of the causeway across Pitsford Water. This is not the main car park at Brixworth Country Park, though that could be used if one wants to use the track to cycle round the reservoir. Kettering station is some 5 miles from Loddington: keep left out of the station, head for the A14/A43 and pick up the B5323, from which a minor road can be followed through Thorpe Malsor. Northampton station is further, but Sustrans Route Six could be followed to pick up signs for Brixworth and Brixworth Country Park. Cycle hire is available from Pitsford Cycles, near the café and visitor centre in the country park. Alternatively, you could park at the memorial on the road between Lamport and Harrington and start from there.

Refreshments: There is a café at Brixworth Country Park, along the traffic-free track beside the reservoir. The Hare, at Loddington (01536 710337), might be a welcome sight after the sharp climb into the village.

The route: Although the lakeside track could be used to extend this route, we do not follow it. After a short climb away from the car park, where there can be quite a bit of traffic, the quiet lanes that follow come as a relief. There are undulations all the way through Draughton. Then a few miles of flat going come to a sharp end before Loddington, where a narrow valley is crossed. More quiet lanes take the route to Walgrave. The closer one gets to Pitsford Water the busier the roads become. There is a cycle-track from Holcot to the end.

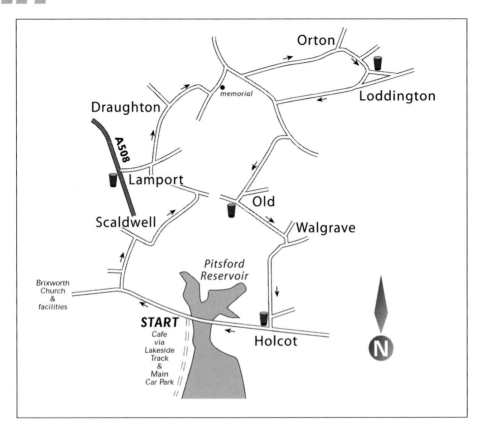

Leave the car park and turn left, up a warming hill. The traffic here can be annoying, but is left behind after 1½ miles. **Turn R** (Scaldwell/Lamport). Follow this road through Scaldwell, passing the old stone houses and the trees that shade the village green. After Scaldwell, **turn L** (Lamport) at a T-junction, to climb steadily to Lamport. The hall and pub are to your left.

At the T-junction, **turn R** (Draughton/Harrington). Very shortly, **turn L** (Draughton). In the tiny village of Draughton, **turn R** (Rothwell). At the end of a gentle climb, at a T-junction, **turn L** (no signpost). A little way further on is a memorial to airmen

of the USAAF. A little way after the memorial, **turn R** (Foxhall/Mawsley/Broughton). After some houses, **turn L** (Orton). Follow this lovely lane through Orton, keeping right at the far end of the village. Before Loddington a narrow valley is crossed. Watch out for the sharp bend and uneven surface at the bottom of the dip. At the top of the hill, **turn R** (Foxhall/Old). Pass through this attractive village to a crossroads near the sports field. **Turn R** (Harrington/Old). This flat road reaches a shaded T-junction. **Turn L** (Old). Still on the flat, **turn R** (Old/Scaldwell). This narrow lane descends almost imperceptibly to Old. On entering Old,

The little village of Draughton

turn R (Walgrave/Lamport) and then, opposite the White Horse, **turn L** (Walgrave/Hannington). Pass through Cherry Hill, to Walgrave. At the crossroads in Walgrave, **turn R** (Holcot/Brixworth). Follow this road to Holcot. At the crossroads, **turn R** (Brixworth – the sign does not come into view until you reach the crossroads). Pick up the cycle track back to the car park – via the lakeside track if you wish to extend the route by about 5 miles.

PITSFORD WATER
A major leisure attraction in this area, with all the necessary facilities for a variety of watersports, gentle, traffic-free cycling and walking, or just sitting around. It can be very busy on sunny weekends. Pitsford Cycles, useful for cycle hire and spares is located near the visitors centre and café, in Brixworth Country Park.

LAMPORT HALL
Another of the impressive stately houses of Northamptonshire, it was the home of the Isham family. *The Diary of Thomas Isham* gives a vivid picture of gentry life in the 17th century. The house contains an impressive library, furniture and paintings. There are good views from the village, especially near the church. The hall hosts a range of special events. Telephone 01604 686272.

BRIXWORTH CHURCH

Brixworth church may not appear especially unusual at first sight, but parts of it date from as early as the 7th century, being founded before the Vikings first came to England. It is described by one architectural historian as the most impressive structure north of the Alps to survive from that century. Much expanded during the following centuries, it was a minster church, which served a wide area and acted as the centre for conversion and the religious life of the region's population. The church is little altered since it was built although there is evidence of damage by Viking raids in the 9th century, and some of the masonry dates from the Roman period so may well have come from a Roman villa that stood close by.

The village of Old

10

Long Buckby, Ashby St Ledgers and Althorp

10 miles or 23 miles

tarting along the B5385, to pass through Watford on the B4036, the route visits Ashby St Ledgers, home of the Gunpowder Plot, and several small villages along very minor roads. Ashby St Ledgers, the Bringtons and Brockhall all have ironstone houses and are particularly attractive. A return is made through the Bringtons, passing close to Althorp House, ancestral home of the Spencer family and last resting place of Diana, Princess of Wales. Many of the roads used are very narrow and quite likely to be free of traffic – though not always – and there are good views throughout.

Map: OS Landranger 152 Northampton and Milton Keynes (GR 627676)

Starting point: This is one of the few routes in the book that could easily be started from a railway station. Long Buckby station is situated less than 1 mile to the south-west of the village: just leave the station and turn right. The route description starts in the village centre. Long Buckby is accessible along the B5385 from either the A5 or A428. Dodford would make an equally good starting point, close to the A45 and A5. There is car parking in the centre of Long Buckby.

Refreshments: Several of the villages have pubs, but there is no shop or pub on the route between Norton and Great Brington, though Little Brington is only slightly off route. The Fox and Hounds at Great Brington (01604 770651), an interesting building, serves food. The White Horse at Norton (01327 702982) is friendly and serves also food. The Old Coach House at Ashby St Ledgers (01788 890349) serves food and drink and is well worth a visit. There are benches outside the village hall at Ashby St Ledgers, which would make an ideal spot to picnic. In Long Buckby, the Old King's Head (01327 844195) is recommended.

The route: The B roads along which the route starts are generally quiet. They undulate all the way to the A5, after which flatter country lanes take over. After Welton the undulations begin again on some very minor lanes. After Norton, there is a certain feeling of being on a helter-skelter. The gated track through Dodford Lodge Farm is officially a road, but the section before the farm is deteriorating and after that it is a mixture of tarmac, potholes and loose gravel. However, it is likely to be devoid of traffic and is quite easily cycled with no more than usual care. More gated roads follow through Brockhall, Althorp and back to Long Buckby.

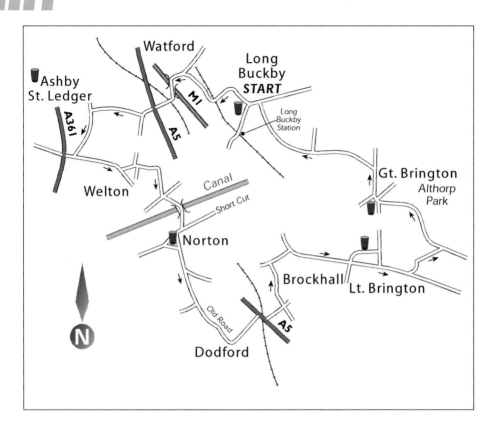

Start in the Market Place in the centre of Long Buckby. Follow the sign to Watford on the B5385. This winds through the village and under the railway line. At the T-junction, **turn L** (Watford B4036). This takes you over the canal, motorway and mainline railway. Soon you reach the A5. Go straight over (Ashby St Ledgers) and soon **turn R** (Ashby St Ledgers). As you approach the village you can see the manor house and church across the fields to the right. The route actually takes the next **L turn**, but Ashby St Ledgers is worth some time. So, follow the road round to the right and enter the village. The manor house and church are close together to the right, but the road to the left is worth a look,

too. The pub is at the far end of the village towards Crick.

Leave Ashby St Ledgers by following the sign to Welton on Cycle Route 70 and retracing your steps. At the sharp left bend, **turn R** (Welton/Daventry/ Cycle Route 70). At the T-junction, close to the A361, **turn L** (Cycle Route 70/Welton). In Welton keep left (Watford). At the crossroads go straight on (no signpost). After a while you will dip down to cross the Grand Union Canal.

*At the next crossroads you could **turn L** (Long Buckby) to return to the start, crossing straight over the A5 and passing Long Buckby station on the way.*

The canal near Welton

The main route goes straight over the crossroads (Norton). At Norton, **turn R** and go gently uphill through the village with the White Horse pub on your right. At the end of the village, **turn L** (Weedon: Weedon Lane). Keep right (Weedon). While descending the hill, the road swings left. As it does, keep to the right (no signpost). This road undulates and the surface becomes poorer. Eventually you come to a gate – the first of several – with a sign saying Dodford Lodge Farm (byway). Go straight on through two more gates to enter the farmyard. Leave it by a fourth gate. Take care of the loose patches and the pot-holes on the descent to Dodford. Throughout this section there are views of Borough Hill, once encumbered by numerous radio masts. How many people can

remember a wireless set with Daventry as one of the stations?

The track swings to the left at the bottom of the hill. The scattered houses of Dodford village are to your right. The church contains one of less than a hundred medieval wooden funeral effigies to be found in England and Wales.

Eventually a properly surfaced road is reached. **Turn L** (no signpost). Before long the A5 is reached. **Turn R** (Weedon), cross the main railway line, and **turn L** (Brockhall). At the next T-junction **turn L** (Brockhall only) and follow the road through this lovely hamlet and exit through two gates. At a third gate, not usually closed, the field on the left was once the site of Muscott village. The farm by the

A fine view of the Nene Valley from near Little Brington

motorway was once the manor house, with moat, gatehouse and fishponds. When the light is at a low angle, the earthworks that appear mark the tracks and peasant houses and crofts. It was deserted because of enclosure for sheep pasture. There are many villages like this in Northamptonshire and the East Midlands.

Follow the road round to the right. Climb the hill and **turn R** (no signpost). Follow this road past the remains of Little Brington church. The tower and spire are all that remain, having been left as a navigation aid for the RAF. There are fine views of the Nene valley from this road. Half a mile later, **turn L** (no signpost, but various restriction signs). A little over 1 mile later, **turn L** (no signpost) through a gate, and follow the road with the wall of Althorp Park on your right. Ahead is Great Brington church, where the Spencer family vaults are housed.

Althorp House is visible from the road, and strikes some as surprisingly modest. Climb the hill to Great Brington and **turn L** (Little Brington/Whilton) and almost immediately, **turn R** (East Haddon/Long Buckby). Great Brington village is to the left. Descend the steep hill, but do not get too much speed up, as near the bottom, just before Hazel Tree House, **turn L** (no signpost) to cross a cattle grid. Follow this narrow road to Long Buckby. At the T-junction, opposite Long Buckby Infants School, **turn L** to arrive in the Market Place. To return to the station, keep straight on.

NORTHAMPTONSHIRE AND THE GUNPOWDER PLOT

The leading light amongst the Gunpowder Plotters, Robert Catesby, was from a well-established Northamptonshire family. Ashby St Ledgers House was theirs. The story goes that it was in the gatehouse that the plot was hatched. William Catesby, five generations before Robert, had been one of Richard III's right-hand men: he was executed after the Battle of Bosworth. Robert's involvement in politics was less formal, but had the same outcome. After the Reformation, Roman Catholics found themselves under increasing suspicion because of supposed joint loyalty to king and Pope. Under pressure from penalties and exclusion from public office, Robert Catesby and his fellow conspirators decided to attempt to destroy their oppressors. Whether they were completely culpable or partly set up in a cynical political manoeuvre, they failed to blow up Parliament and King James I and VI with it. It is interesting to reflect that it is a failure that we celebrate on 5th November. Another local family involved in the plot were the Treshams: Francis, son of Thomas Tresham, the builder, seems to have played a double role. On the one hand, he was amongst the plotters, but he was also related through marriage to Lord Mounteagle who received a warning letter. Francis was the only one of the plotters not to die immediately after the plot, but suffered a mysterious death in the Tower of London a little later. (See route 5)

ALTHORP AND THE SPENCERS

The Spencer family rose to prominence through the profits from their sheep pastures. Althorp was bought originally for that purpose. Supplemented by the profits of public service from the reign of Henry VIII onwards, they have not looked back. Althorp House is, surprisingly, not one of the grandest in the country. The Earls Spencer seem to have preferred, wisely given the fate of so many stately homes, elegance and homeliness to grandeur. It has a suitably interesting history to match its collections. Charles I came, from Holdenby, to play bowls whilst under arrest at the end of the Civil War. Spencer influence was great enough to control the election of MPs in Northampton borough for many years. In the reign of Victoria, Gladstone would have recommended the fifth Earl Spencer as his successor as Prime Minister: unfortunately the Queen was not on speaking terms with Mr. Gladstone. When the nearby railway line was built, it had to have gullies and bridges so that important business – fox hunting – was not disturbed. Add to this a private waiting room at the station and the right to stop any train they pleased and you get the picture of Spencer prominence. However, they have remained popular in the county. Most recently Diana, Princess of Wales was laid to rest in the grounds of her ancient family home. The traditional place of rest for the Spencers was Great Brington church, where the memorials may be seen. Althorp House is open to the public, for information call 01604 770017 or visit www.althorp.com.

(11)

Castle Ashby and Wollaston

5 miles or 14 miles

Stately Castle Ashby dominates this area visually and as an estate. In some ways it sits ill alongside small industrial towns such as Wollaston. On the other hand, this contrast is typical of Northamptonshire. For the cyclist, quiet country lanes are ideal for a short trip. Easton Maudit has a remarkable tree trunk opposite the church and inside the church is the tomb of Sir Simon Yelvertoft, author of the House of Commons prayer. How successful his work has been is left up to you to decide.

Map: OS Landranger 152 Northampton and Milton Keynes (GR 866602)

Starting point: This route could be started at Castle Ashby, where there is a car park. However, to make the last leg downhill, the route has been described from any of the several parking places near the lakes along the Grendon to Castle Ashby road. Wollaston is the nearest point on the route to Wellingborough railway station. This would involve a ride of some 5 miles, first along the B573 and then the A509, to the roundabout near Wollaston. A right turn could be made there for Grendon. Grendon and Castle Ashby are both easily accessible and signposted from the A45, between Northampton and Wellingborough, or the A509 or A428.

Refreshments: The Buttery in the 'country shopping' courtyard at Castle Ashby serves food and drink. The Falcon Hotel, Castle Ashby (01604 696200) and the Half Moon, in Grendon (01933 663263), both serve the needs of cyclists, with the Falcon being rather more upmarket.

The route: From the popular lakes between Castle Ashby and Grendon, the route goes uphill to Castle Ashby, where it picks up a series of lanes that pass amongst the fields and woods to Wollaston and back to the start via Grendon. There are undulations throughout, but the steepest bits are downward. The route is almost entirely on minor roads, the busiest part being the crossing of the A509 at a roundabout near Wollaston.

From any of the parking places near the lakes, **turn L**. Follow the road, with views up to Castle Ashby House and church on a hill across the lakes. At the T-junction, **turn L** (Castle Ashby). As the road levels out at the top of the hill, **turn L** (Village/Easton Maudit) to pass the Falcon Hotel. Almost immediately **turn L** (no signpost) and keep left. The lakes will now appear to be straight ahead. Follow this road as it sweeps below

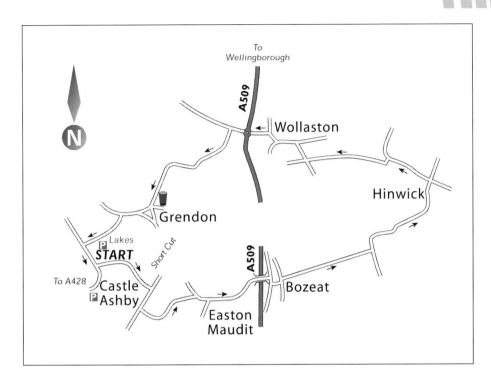

Castle Ashby House and then ascends, passing some attractive farm buildings before reaching a T-junction. *The route could be shortened here by turning left and then left again for Grendon, to rejoin the main route.*

For the main route, **turn R** (Yardley Hastings). About ¼ mile later, **turn L** (no signpost). The road descends, crosses a tiny stream and then ascends. Follow it as it sweeps to the left with the spires of Easton Maudit and Bozeat churches ahead. At the T-junction, **turn R** (Easton Maudit/Bozeat). Pass the ancient tree trunk and church in Easton Maudit, carrying straight on for Bozeat. After crossing a bridge over the A509 bypass, the road descends and veers sharply to the left, **turn R** (Village Only) into London Road. Almost immediately **turn L** (no

signpost) into Mile Street. This becomes Church Lane. At the T-junction, **turn L** (no signpost). *(Turning right here will take you to a shop.)* Almost immediately **turn R** (Hinwick/Harrold/Podington). Follow this almost straight road to a T-junction and **turn L** (Hinwick/Podington). This tree-lined road skirts Hinwick and passes Hinwick Hall. At the crossroads next to the Hall, **turn L** (Wollaston). Where the road bears sharply right, **turn L** (Wollaston) with long views of the Nene Valley ahead. At a crossroads in a dip, **turn R** (Irchester). At the T-junction, **turn L** (Wollaston/Bozeat) onto the B569. In Wollaston, at the end of the long brick wall, **turn R** (Lorries A509) into Bell End. Descend to the roundabout at the bottom of the hill. Go straight across (Grendon/Great Doddington). Shortly, **turn L** (Grendon). In

The grounds of Castle Ashby are open to the public

Grendon, pass the Half Moon and go up the hill. Immediately after the church **turn R** (Castle Ashby/Earls Barton) into Church Way. Keep right at the grassy triangle and **turn R** (no signpost) at the T- junction into Station Road. Immediately after a small bridge, **turn L** (Castle Ashby/Denton). This is the road that runs alongside the lakes.

CASTLE ASHBY

Castle Ashby is still the centre of a major estate of some 10,000 acres. It first became so when Sir William Compton, from an old Warwickshire family, was well rewarded for growing up with and serving Henry VIII. He bought Ashby David, Yardley Hastings and six other nearby manors. Later Ashby David became Castle Ashby and the Comptons became Earls of Northampton. The grounds, laid out by Capability Brown, are open daily to the public: a notice at the car park gives details. There is 'country shopping' and a plant centre. The views all round are very good. The house is not open to the public (it is a venue for conferences, weddings and 'events' rather than a home), but the outside can easily be seen. On summer weekends, cricket is sometimes played on the tree-fringed field near the house. Castle Ashby has a website, www.castleashby.co.uk.

THE BOOT AND SHOE BELT

Wollaston is typical of many small towns or large villages along the boot and shoe belt. They expanded rapidly during the 19th century. At that time much of the manufacturing process was not mechanised: it did not become so until the 20th century, and even then not fully. Wollaston, associated with the Griggs family and the Doc Marten brand, was close enough to the railway lines to prosper. Northampton, once the capital of shoe production, was challenged by Kettering and Leicester as shoe manufacture spread eastwards. The opening of a railway line from London to Leicester helped shift manufacture to this area of Northamptonshire.

The imposing Hinwick Hall is passed on the way

12

Salcey Forest and Yardley Chase

11 miles, 19 miles or 22 miles

Variety is the spice of this route, passing through what was once royal forest, skirting the Nene Valley, visiting the 'prodigy house' of the Marquess of Northampton at Castle Ashby and crossing Yardley Chase before heading back to the start. The neat manor and tiny church at little Preston Deanery; the elegant church of Whiston standing prominently on a spur; the mellow estate buildings of Castle Ashby, and the stone cottages of Yardley Hastings, are the village highlights of this pocket tour of the country to the south-east of Northampton. In summer, the slopes of the Nene Valley often have fields of pick-your-own soft fruit: take a basket!

Map: OS Landranger 152 Northampton and Milton Keynes (GR 793518)

Starting point: Salcey Forest Visitor Centre is 6 miles south-east of Northampton, close to the M1. Follow signs for Hartwell and Salcey Forest from the A508 at Roade or for Salcey Forest from the B526 between Horton and Stoke Goldington. There is a car park, information, toilets and a café. Castle Ashby would make an equally good starting point. The nearest railway stations are at Northampton and Wolverton, though neither is conveniently close to Salcey Forest. Great Houghton is the closest point on the ride to Northampton station, about 4 miles away. Follow Sustrans Cycle Route Six through the town centre to Great Houghton. Similarly, Sustrans Route Six could be followed from Wolverton station: head through Hanslope and Long Street, for Salcey Forest. However, this would add about 10 miles each way.

Refreshments: There are cafés at Salcey Forest and in the country shopping courtyard at Castle Ashby, The Buttery (01604 696728). The Falcon Hotel (01604 696200) at Castle Ashby is an up-market establishment. The nearest pub to the start is the Rose and Crown (01604 862393) at Hartwell. Its namesake (01604 696276) at Yardley Hastings also makes for a good stopping point.

The route: Quiet lanes lead up to the valley of the Nene at Great Houghton, from where there is a rapid descent through the village. A very short stretch of the A428 is used – there is a path to use if you wish. The route then undulates to Cogenhoe for another rapid descent. A narrow lane climbs through Whiston, with its prominent church, on the way to Castle Ashby. More lanes are followed before a cycle track is used to avoid riding on the A428 between Yardley Hastings and Denton. The route then returns to Salcey Forest via lanes and a 2-mile section of the B526 – possibly the busiest road used on any of the routes in this book.

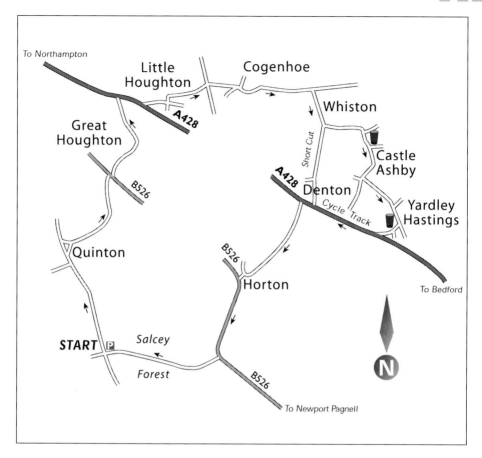

From the car park at the Salcey Forest visitor centre, **turn R**. Some 2 miles later, **turn R** (Quinton/Preston Deanery). Pass through both of these to a crossroads. Take care here. Go straight over (Great Houghton). Descend through Great Houghton to the A428. **Turn R** (Bedford). There is no official cycle track here but the road is rarely busy outside peak periods. However, there is a path on the far side of the road if you wish to push your bike for a short stretch. Shortly, **turn L** (Little Houghton). In Little Houghton, **turn L** at the crossroads by the church (Cogenhoe). There are views over the

Nene Valley and the inland resort at Billing Aquadrome.

At a staggered crossroads, **turn L** and immediately **turn R** (Cogenhoe/Grendon). Pass through Cogenhoe. The older part of the village is down Church Street. From there a bridleway can be followed down to Cogenhoe Mill, a pleasant spot on the River Nene. On the main route, freewheel down a steep hill. **Turn R** (Whiston/Castle Ashby). Whiston church stands elegantly on the skyline.

Just after Whiston you could shorten the

There are lovely views around Little Houghton

*route and miss out Castle Ashby. **Turn R** for Denton (signpost missing at present), then follow this road to the left in the village to rejoin the main route at the A428.*

The main route carries straight on for Castle Ashby village. Pass through it. Soon **turn L** (Yardley Hastings). *(Ignoring this left turn will take you directly to the cycle track by the A428.)* In Yardley Hastings, **turn R** (Denton/Northampton). Shortly, **keep R** along Northampton Road. As the main road comes into view, get onto the cycle track on the path on the right-hand side of the A428 (Denton/Northampton). The main route follows the cycle track, nearly to Denton. Yardley Hastings lies off the A428 and has quiet, twisting lanes,

some old houses and, on the main road, shops.

Just before Denton, carefully cross the A428. You could use the path on the far side, too. **Turn L** (Horton/Hackleton) to skirt the edge of Yardley Chase. In Horton, **turn L** (Horton) and, shortly, **turn L** (Stoke Goldington/Newport Pagnell) onto the B526. This is generally fairly quiet, but at peak times it can be quite busy. After 2 miles on this road **turn R** (Salcey Forest/Hartwell/Hanslope). Follow this road to a crossroads and **turn R** (Quinton) to return to the Visitor Centre, on the right.

● ●

SALCEY FOREST
Before the 18th century much of

Northamptonshire was wooded. The term 'forest', though, did not equate to woodland. Whittlewood, Rockingham and Salcey Forests were areas subject to Forest Law, which reserved them for hunting wild beasts by the monarch and meted out harsh punishments to anyone else. The timber was less important than the animals: ordinary folk had the right to use the wood, so long as they followed the custom of what they could use and when. Later on, the wood was in great demand for shipbuilding and charcoal. Timber was also cleared for agricultural improvement. Salcey Forest, now a fraction of its original size, is a leisure amenity for all and an important habitat for wildlife. There is a variety of waymarked walks and rides (cyclists may use surfaced tracks) and more are being developed. There are notice-boards with information on routes, special events and wildlife and also a tree-top walkway.

YARDLEY CHASE

Yardley Chase was in the extensive Royal Forest. It is an important area for wildlife, despite, or maybe due to being largely out of bounds to the public. During the Second World War it served as a huge ammunition depot, with its own railway line, and some of the buildings remain. A small area is still used by the services for training.

Halfway round the route, Yardley Hastings makes a good stopping point

13
Mears Ashby Figure of Eight
10 miles, 14 miles or 24 miles

For some reason I find Mears Ashby a complicated place to navigate round and could ride a figure of eight in the village before finding my way out. Not such a bad thing as it is a pretty village with houses from most periods since the 17th century and narrow, twisting lanes around the church. Sywell and Holcot are attractive spots, while Hannington and Orlingbury provide oases of quiet close to major towns. Any turning in Ecton might lead to interesting buildings behind the two lines of stone houses that flank the steep high street. The church at Earls Barton is renowned, dominating the crossroads at the heart of this big village. There are wide views over the Nene, before a turning is made to Wilby for a return to the start through more gentle countryside.

Maps: OS Landranger 152 Northampton and Milton Keynes and 141 Kettering and Corby (GR 838666)

Starting point: There is no ideal starting point, as regards parking. There is a car park at Sywell Country Park, sheet 152 (GR 834652), but this would mean a ferocious uphill start. There is plentiful on-street parking in Mears Ashby, but please be sure not to leave a car anywhere where it may cause an obstruction.

Refreshments: The Griffin's Head, Mears Ashby (01604 812945), is easily missed, so keep an eye out. The Lamb at Little Harrowden (01933 673300) is passed on the route. The Apotho Coffee Shop (01604 810289) is in the centre of Earls Barton. Basic refreshments from the shop at Sywell Country Park.

The route: The loop of eight to the north, via Sywell, Hannington and Orlingbury is 14 miles. The southern loop via Ecton and Earls Barton is shorter, but hillier. Close proximity to Northampton and Wellingborough does not preclude quiet cycling, though you might find more traffic than on other minor roads at peak times. On the southern loop there is a goodly down and up near Sywell Country Park. The road is narrow, so take special care of cars on this section. After Ecton, an off-road section starts unpromisingly, but soon becomes a cart track. Earls Barton and Wilby are both at the top of hills. There are short stretches of A road and B road, but most of the route is on minor roads.

Start at Mears Ashby church, at the junction of Vicarage Lane and Church Street. With your back to the church go left along Church Street. At the T-junction, **turn L** (no signpost) into North Street. Follow this road round to the left (Earls Barton). At the crossroads, **turn R** (Sywell

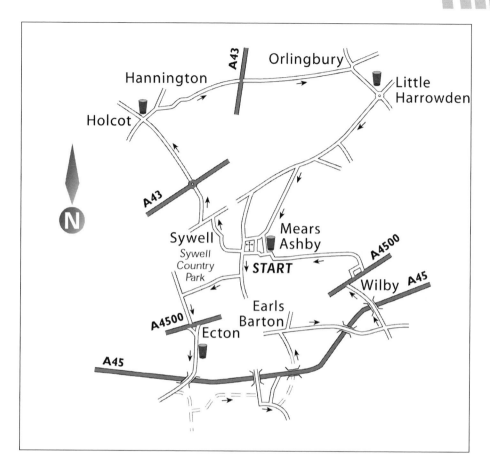

Airport/Overstone). After a quick descent and a slower ascent, reach Sywell. Pass the church and at the T-junction, **turn L** (Overstone). Almost immediately, at a mini-roundabout **turn R** (Holcot) into Holcot Road. This road skirts Sywell airport. At the roundabout on the A43, much less busy here than to the south-west of Northampton, go straight over (Holcot/Brixworth). When entering Holcot, watch out for the various waterfowl that wander across the road. At the crossroads, **turn R** (Walgrave/Old) to pass the White Swan. On leaving Holcot, **turn R**

(Hannington). Follow this road through Hannington, passing the church that seems to be too wide for its tower. Soon the A43 is re-crossed by going straight on (Isham/Orlingbury) at the crossroads near a garage. On reaching Orlingbury village green, **turn R** (Little Harrowden/Wellingborough). A quick descent leads to Little Harrowden, where one goes uphill, passing the Lamb, to a roundabout. At the roundabout, **turn R** (Hardwick/Sywell/Mears Ashby). Ignore the first two left turns for Wellingborough. Then, where the road

The tower of All Saints' church in Earls Barton dates from Saxon times

turns sharp right, **turn L** (Mears Ashby). Follow this road back to the village. At the T-junction, **turn R** (Sywell) into North Street. *To return to the church **turn L** (no signpost) into Church Street.*

The main route does not turn into Church Street, but continues towards Earls Barton. Leave Mears Ashby and after a while, **turn R** (Sywell Country Park). The road descends steeply past the entrance to the park and climbs equally steeply up the other side of the valley. At the T-junction, **turn L** (Ecton). Shortly cross the main road into a one-way street, to enter Ecton. At the T-junction, **turn L** (no signpost) into High Street.

Descend along the main street with lovely stone houses on either side and pass the Three Horseshoes. The lines of houses are replaced by lines of trees as you leave the village. Immediately after crossing the bridge over the A45, **turn L** (byway) on a rough track, passing by a barrier. Keep right as the trees are approached. The surface is rough, but easily cycled. Where the track meets another track, **turn L** (no signpost). The A45 is not visible, but it can be heard, and the track runs parallel to it. Eventually, go under a footbridge and up an incline on a tarmac surface to reach a T-junction. **Turn R** (no signpost). Ignore the slip road to the A45. Immediately before the no entry signs at the end of the exit slip road, **turn L** onto a rough track (Pocket Park). Negotiate the barrier – you'll probably need to get off. Go through a subway under the A45 and then keep left up an old road. Earls Barton church is straight ahead.

At the crossroads in the centre of Earls Barton, **turn R** (Great Doddington/Wellingborough). Cross the bridge over the A45. At a crossroads, **turn L** (Wilby/Wellingborough Rugby Club). Cross a bridge over the A45, for the last time. A rapid descent is followed by a sharp climb into Wilby. At the T-junction **turn R** (no signpost) onto Main Street. After a short while, just before signs warning of traffic lights, **turn L** (no signpost) into Church Lane. Bear right at the church and very soon, at the T-junction **turn L** (no signpost). (If you miss Church Lane, just continue to the next left,

signposted Mears Ashby.) Follow this road to Mears Ashby. At the four-way junction, keep straight ahead and pass the Griffin's Head. As the road starts to descend, **turn R** (no signpost) into Ladies Lane. Keep right at the church and immediately reach the junction of Vicarage Lane and Church Street.

• •

CHURCHES

Hannington church looks oddly proportioned: inside, the nave is split into two. All this comes down to Gilbert of Sempringham, founder of the Gilbertine Order – the only monastic order to originate in England. Unusually, the order was for monks and nuns: it seems that each had one half of the church in their monasteries. They controlled Hannington church and it was built in their style.

The tower of Earls Barton church is one of

Waterfowl are likely to wander across the road near Holcot

the best examples of Anglo-Saxon architecture in England, strongly resembling designs used by some kings on their coinage. It is likely that the first place of worship was in the ground floor of the tower. Before the Norman Conquest, the church would have dominated the surrounding collection of thatched huts, and it probably provided both a physical as well as a spiritual refuge for the inhabitants in times of trouble.

SYWELL AERODROME

While cycling the northern loop of this ride, you are likely to see a variety of aircraft overhead from this private aerodrome, opened by local enthusiasts in 1928. Before the Second World War it was used for pilot training, and during the war both RAF airmen and Free-French were trained there. It was also a base for repairs to bomber aircraft, thus making a major contribution to the war effort. In 2001 a group of volunteers started a museum there. They point out that, 'it is no Hendon or Duxford', but it does contain private collections of artifacts, and memorabilia and material from local airfields. For details of their limited opening hours, visit www.sywellaerodrome.co.uk. The clubhouse, mess and other original buildings are now a restaurant and hotel.

Sywell

14

Blisworth and Weedon

7 miles, 15 miles or 22½ miles

Starting on a hillside near the Grand Union Canal, this route heads for Blisworth, with its famous canal tunnel, before following quiet lanes through a series of pretty villages (Litchborough and Farthingstone have some impressive ironstone houses just off the main route) to Weedon. Here, all the great routes from London to the north-west run within a few yards of one another. Roman roads, coaching inns, main line railways, the Grand Union Canal and the M1: this is much travelled country. The lanes around Litchborough, Preston Capes and Everdon, to the west of this route, are well worth exploring, too.

Map: OS Landranger 152 Northampton and Milton Keynes (GR 717554).

Starting point: Use the car park near the canal bridge on the road between Milton Malsor and Gayton. This is accessible from the A43 by turning for Blisworth. In Blisworth turn right at the bottom of the hill and left at the Royal Oak. When the road turns sharp right, turn left into Northampton Road. Just before reaching Milton Malsor turn left signposted Rothersthorpe and Gayton. Immediately after the bridge over the A43 turn left. The car park is just after the second canal bridge. From other directions pick up the signs at Milton Malsor, which can be reached from the A45 at Northampton. It is about 6 miles from Northampton station. If you use an off road bike, you could always follow the Northampton Arm of the canal to Blisworth Arm, which the route passes through.

Refreshments: There are probably more pubs on this route than any other in the guide. Just off the route in Middle Lane in Nether Heyford (turn left after the village shop), the Old Sun is popular with cyclists. The Red Lion at Litchborough (01327 830250) is cosy and welcoming but does not, at present, serve food. The Royal Oak at Blisworth (01604 858372) serves a good pint and does serve food. Weedon has a café, Granny's Kitchen (01327 340040) as well as pubs.

The route: There are lots of hills on this route, both up and down, on the way to Weedon. Some are steep, but none are long. Main roads are crossed, but the main route is entirely on minor roads. The canal towpath can be used on the return journey. It is accessible from Weedon onwards, though it is only recommended after dry weather and with suitable tyres. There is no towpath through the Blisworth tunnel. Alternative starting places could be Blisworth or Weedon. Parking is not easy in Blisworth, though there is a small car park at the northern portal of the tunnel, reached off Stoke Road, after following signs for Stoke Bruerne.

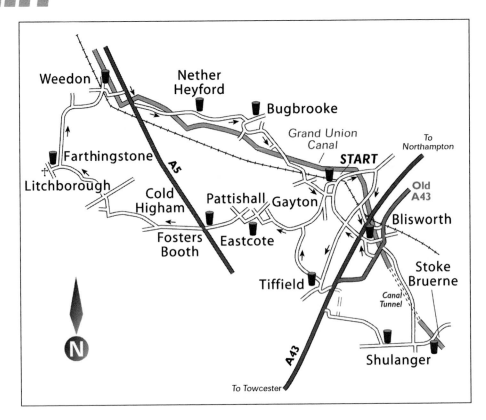

Turn L (no signpost) out of the car park. Where the road bears sharp left, **turn R** (Blisworth Arm) and pass over a narrow hump-backed bridge to pass the canal buildings and junction. After two more bridges, the last over the railway, **turn L** (Blisworth). Follow this road past the Walnut Tree Inn, formerly the Blisworth Station Hotel, for nearly a mile and **turn R** (Blisworth) along the old A43. In the village **turn R** (Towcester) at the T-junction. **Turn R** (Towcester) at the Royal Oak, and pass the post office and church before reaching the bridge over the canal at the former mill. *The tunnel is easily accessible by turning left along the well-surfaced towpath.*
The main route continues over the

bridge, ignoring the left turn for Towcester, instead **turn R** (Gayton), to pass around the back of the mill. **Turn L** (no signpost) at the next T-junction. Follow this road over the A43, then **turn L** (Tiffield). In Tiffield, before reaching the George Inn, **turn R** (Eastcote).

After a mile, at a T-junction, **turn L** (Eastcote). *(To head back to the start, **turn R** for Gayton, rejoining the main route there.)* **Turn L** again (Eastcote). **Turn L** (Foster's Booth) at the crossroads, after the Eastcote Arms. At the next T-junction, **turn R** (Pattishall/Foster's Booth). At the crossroads **turn L** (Foster's Booth: Butchers Lane). There is a pub and a

Candle Bridge, Blisworth

restaurant on the A5. Once the Roman road from London to the north-west, this later became a route for stage-coaches. The hilly section north of Towcester required extra horses. These were changed it seems, by a man called Foster who had his booth here.

Cross the A5 (Cold Higham: Banbury Lane). In St Luke's church in Cold Higham is one of less than 100 medieval wooden funeral effigies in England. **Turn R** (Litchborough). Litchborough has some pretty buildings and the green by the church is a good spot for a break. In Litchborough, go across the staggered crossroads (Farthingstone).

*To head back to the start, **turn R** in Litchborough and follow the signs to Bugbrooke, to rejoin the main route by turning right after crossing the canal. On*

this short-cut there is a monument to Robert Watson Watt, who led the development of radar for tracking aircraft in the 1930s. They used the hill behind for their tests. This development proved vital during the Second World War.

In Farthingstone, the King's Arms, opposite the church, is one of several beautiful buildings. In the village, **turn R** (The Stowes/Weedon). Follow this road to Weedon. Along the way there are fine views of Arbury Hill, Borough Hill and of Weedon Barracks.

In Weedon, **turn R** at the crossroads by the Plume of Feathers (no signpost). *To take a closer look at the barracks don't turn right, but carry straight on, then retrace your steps.*

The main road passes under the railway and canal. You could get up to the

Weedon Barracks were built to shelter VIPs should Napoleon have invaded Britain

canal and follow the towpath all the way to Blisworth (see section overleaf on towpath option). At the A5 **turn R** (Foster's Booth/Towcester), using the cycle track. **Turn L** (Nether Heyford) after the Narrow Boat pub.

In Nether Heyford follow signs for Bugbrooke. At the first junction go straight on, **turn R** at the next give way sign and then **turn R** again.

At a T-junction **turn R** (Litchborough). Shortly, **turn L** (Village Only) where the main road veers sharply to the right. Follow this road to emerge at a grassy triangle with a telephone box in the middle and a general stores on the right. **Turn R** (no signpost). After ½ mile carry straight on, as signposted, for Blisworth and Gayton. Re-cross the canal and railway to go over a staggered crossroads, for Gayton and Blisworth.

At the crossroads in Gayton **turn L** (no signpost – the only direction that does not have one) to pass the Queen Victoria and the Eykyn Arms. **Turn L** at the next T-junction (no signpost) and follow the road round to the right, with grand views over the Nene Valley to the left. At the church, where there is another of the unusual wooden effigies mentioned elsewhere, **turn L** to descend carefully to the car park.

● ●

BLISWORTH TO STOKE BRUERNE

To get to Stoke Bruerne from Blisworth follow the signs to Stoke Bruerne from near the Royal Oak. You could return to Blisworth by the same route, or head for Shutlanger, turn right at the Plough, follow the road past an isolated farm to turn right onto a roughly surfaced bridleway. Bear left at a farmyard and reach the A43. This is a fast and busy road. Cross with care. After that, head either to Tiffield or Blisworth and retrace your steps to the car park at the start. There is now a cycle track from the Showsley junction to the Blisworth turn, alongside the A43.

THE CANAL TOWPATH
At any convenient point, Weedon or Blisworth can be reached along the canal towpath. There are sections where the surface is very poor and some where it is very good. Wide tyres are recommended. Where the surface is soft, please be prepared to walk and preserve the path. I have not described all access points, so make sure you head in the right direction! You need to switch to the opposite side of the canal at bridge 47, then, at Blisworth Arm where a branch of the canal heads to Northampton, you should go up to the road, cross over the bridge and regain the towpath on the other side. Shortly after passing through Blisworth you will come to the northern portal of the Blisworth Tunnel.

BLISWORTH AND STOKE BRUERNE
Nowadays a picturesque village, Stoke Bruerne hides a busy industrial past. The main street was re-orientated along the line of the canal. Information about the impact of the building of the canal can be found on display boards and in the museum. Blisworth does not have the same tourist congestion as Stoke Bruerne, but was equally industrialised. Between 1800 and 1805 the two villages were the busiest inland ports in Britain. The tunnel

between the two villages took much longer to complete than was originally envisaged: poor materials, rudimentary geological techniques and corrupt or negligent contractors all caused problems. In the meantime, all goods had to be hauled over the hill on wagons. However, in 1805, the tunnel completed the quickest route for goods between London and the West Midlands. Soldiers were embarked on barges from Blisworth during the Napoleonic Wars and even Pickfords had a wharf. In the early days of the railways Blisworth had an important station: a traveller from Manchester to Norwich would have changed there, to catch a stagecoach. The Canal Museum at Stoke Bruerne is located in an old mill (01604 862229), has displays and runs activities. Recently Blisworth Heritage Society has developed self-guided walks and there are information boards that outline the interesting past of the village.

WEEDON
The original village of Weedon was up on the hill. Later it spread down the slopes as Weedon Bec and then Road Weedon. From late Saxon times it stood at the crossroads of Watling Street and the Portway, which linked Northampton and Coventry. During the stagecoach era, it acted as a service station. Weedon Barracks was originally built for the government to retreat to should Napoleon have landed his troops in Britain – it was at the centre of the communications network of the time.

15

Canons Ashby to Badby

12 or 19 miles (20 miles including Fawsley Hall)

The western edge of Northamptonshire has lovely countryside, lots of quiet lanes and, in Canons Ashby, a gem in the crown of the National Trust. Great estates once dominated the area: Fawsley and Catesby are visited on this trip. Many of the villages are much smaller than they were in the 15th century, having been enclosed as sheep pasture when landowners realised they could make more money from wool than arable farming. This is really a ride through a deserted landscape. Keep eyes peeled for signs of what was once there. Views change frequently as the route winds around spurs of hills and in and out of valleys. The scenery is excellent throughout. In April and May many of the woods are full of bluebells, with Badby Woods, to the south-east of the village, particularly renowned as a sea of blue.

Maps: OS Landranger 151 Stratford on Avon (just), and 152 Northampton and Milton Keynes. Badby (GR 560590) and Canons Ashby (GR 576505) are on sheet 152.

Starting point: Badby is an attractive village, off the A361 3 miles south of Daventry. There is street parking, though please take care not to block entrances. Canons Ashby would make an equally good starting point, with Badby or Hellidon for a refreshment break. There is a car park at Canons Ashby but the village is not as accessible as Badby, being equidistant from main roads, although is well signposted.

Refreshments: The Red Lion Inn (01327 261200) at Hellidon is a fine place to break the journey, whilst the Windmill at Badby (01327 702363) is conveniently on the route through the village. The Maltsters Arms (01327 702905), on the village green in Badby, is not on the route, but is worth seeking out. Apart from that there is a café at Canons Ashby House. This is open when the house is open (see below), and you do not need to pay to enter the house to use the café. There are no other opportunities for refreshments on this route.

The route: This route is all on minor roads, some very minor, though it crosses the A361 twice. This is hilly country, but we encounter steady climbs rather than steep ascents. The big hill is at Preston Capes and this heads downwards. The section close to Canons Ashby is flatter than the rest, but none is without hills for long.

Canons Ashby to Badby: **turn L** out of the car park and **turn L** at the T-junction. Pass to the left of the church and as you pass the house,

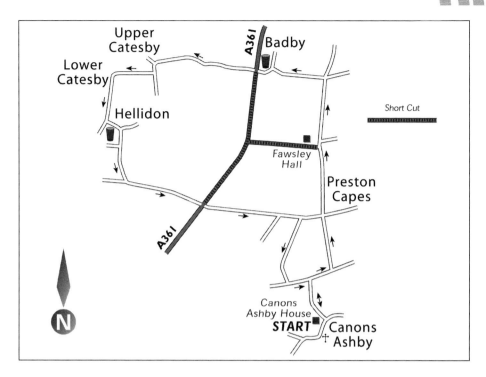

turn L (Preston Capes/Cycle Route 70). At the T-junction, **turn R** (Little Preston/Route 70).

Turn L (Preston Capes/Newnham/ Route 70). Two miles from the start go straight on at crossroads in Preston Capes, into High Street (Newnham/Route 70).

The road descends and then undulates, flanked by trees and with masses of wildflowers in spring. At the next cross-roads go straight on (Newnham/Route 70), unless you want to detour to Fawsley Park, which is well worth doing, in which case **turn L** at the crossroads (Fawsley/Charwelton). Fawsley Park is a pleasant place to stroll or sit and picnic, but please remember that it is privately owned. *For a shorter route back to Canons Ashby, follow this*

*road through Fawsley to the A361, **turn L** for a short distance, **turn L** at the crossroads (Preston Capes/Canons Ashby) then follow the main route from there to Canons Ashby.*

To resume the main route from Fawsley, retrace your steps to the crossroads and **turn L** (Newnham/Route 70). Head towards Newnham until you reach another crossroads, **turn L** (Badby). This gated road is narrow and rough in places. Keep straight on to Badby. **Turn L** onto Main Street.

Badby to Canons Ashby: head up Main Street, passing the post office and the Windmill pub on the right. Keep right into Bunkers Hill (short but vengeful). Soon, cross the busy A361 at the crossroads, heading straight on (Catesby). Don't worry if you get the

Along the lane from Catesby

impression that the road had disappeared into a farmyard, just keep going straight on: it *is* a road. At the T-junction, **turn L** (Lower Catesby/Hellidon). Ignore the next right (a cul de sac). **Turn R** (Lower Catesby).

Go down the hill to Lower Catesby, keeping left at the remarkable coach house. Follow this road to the edge of Hellidon and **turn L** (Charwelton). At the T-junction, by the Red Lion, **turn R** (Priors Marston/Byfield). Soon you will see a sign pointing straight on to Charwelton. At the T-junction, **turn L** (Charwelton/Preston Capes). Keep straight on to cross the A361 (Preston Capes/Canons Ashby). It says it is 8 miles to Canons Ashby, it is less by our route. *(To make a shorter return to Badby, **turn L** on the A361 and **turn R** on the narrow lane that passes Fawsley*

Hall and rejoin the route by turning left at the crossroads (Newnham/Route 70.) On the main route, **turn R** at the second right at the top of the hill (Eydon). At the T-junction **turn L** (no signpost) to pass Northwest Farm. Shortly, **turn R** (Canons Ashby). Follow it to Canons Ashby House.

● ●

DESERTED VILLAGES

Northamptonshire and its neighbouring counties have many deserted village sites and other shrunken villages. People still live in Church Charwelton, Fawsley, Catesby and Canons Ashby, but in fewer numbers than there were in the late Middle Ages. The Black Death of 1348-49 is often identified as the cause of desertion. However, the booming wool business of the 14th to 16th centuries encouraged landowners to clear the peasants off the land and enclose their fields for sheep pasture. Where the people went is not known and was probably not of much concern to the lord of the manor. All they have left behind are groups of rectangular banks and ditches showing where their 'tofts and crofts' were, and the ridge and furrow made by their ploughs. These can be seen easily from the air, but can also be distinguished when the sun is low. At Fawsley it was the Knightley family who enclosed the two villages there, leaving an isolated church and a beautiful manor house with a magnificent oriel window. After 1175 Catesby was owned by a Cistercian nunnery. In 1495, fourteen houses were pulled down and, 22 years later, 60 more people were evicted. There is now but little to show of what was once there.

CANONS ASHBY

The eponymous canons were Black Canons, a celibate religious order following the rule of St Augustine. The remaining parts of the church and surrounding earthworks can still be seen. The well, in a small building in a field to the north of the church, was built by them around 1253 and was later used to supply water to the house until the 1920s; hollowed out tree trunks were used to carry the water. Having enclosed the land for sheep pasture, the priory was itself dissolved in 1536 by Henry VIII, and it came into the possession of John Cope, a member of a prominent Puritan family. Around 1573, the Drydens came into possession through marriage and started to build the present house. Over the years it was extended as finance allowed, and this is the charm of Canons Ashby. Today's visitor now gets to see a charming hotch-potch full of original features that have, elsewhere, been destroyed. A fine place to have a break, to start or to finish. For further information, go to www.nationaltrust.org.uk or telephone 01327 860044.

Canons Ashby is worth exploring

16

Boddington and The Welsh Road

9 miles or 16 miles (20 including Wormleighton)

The Warwickshire–Northamptonshire border provides many miles of quiet cycling. The hills are generally on the Northamptonshire side, so there are often fine views over the flatter fields of Warwickshire. The villages are off the beaten track: tourists around here head for Stratford-on-Avon! This is a route for peace and quiet. In springtime, the fields are full of lambs, as they have been for centuries. Priors Marston and Wormleighton are just in Warwickshire. Wormleighton has a beautiful, hidden-away church and manor house. Boddington Pool is a good spot to sit in the sun and do nothing in particular. All round a sleepy sort of route in the peace of the heart of England.

Maps: OS Landranger 151 Stratford–on-Avon (GR 494535). About 300 yards are on OS Landranger 152.

Starting point: Boddington reservoir lies between Byfield and Upper Boddington. It is reached from Byfield on the A361 or by following signs to Wormleighton and Boddington from the A423. There is parking on the Byfield and Boddington sides of the reservoir, which is popular with anglers.

Refreshments: There are pubs in Upper and Lower Boddington, Byfield and Priors Marston. They are not always open, so go well supplied. Have a picnic at Boddington Pool, on the green in Priors Marston or under a tree at Wormleighton. There is a village shop in Upper Boddington.

The route: This route is entirely on minor roads, though it does cross the A361. A short stretch is in Warwickshire. There are one or two ups, especially to the east of the A361, but the only really steep hill is the one descending into Priors Marston. It is possible to shorten the distance by nearly half by carrying straight on, at the crossroads, after Byfield to get back to the reservoir.

Leave the car park and **turn L** (no signpost). Ignore the sign for Lower Boddington, go into Upper Boddington and **turn L** (shop/post office) after the Plough Inn. This soon becomes Church Road. Go past the shop and the church, with good views to the right. In Lower Boddington **turn L** at the crossroads by the Carpenters Arms (Aston le Walls).

In Aston le Walls, go straight on (Culworth/Sulgrave/Chipping Warden). Continue straight on at crossroads with the A361 (Culworth). (This route does not go to Culworth, but it is an

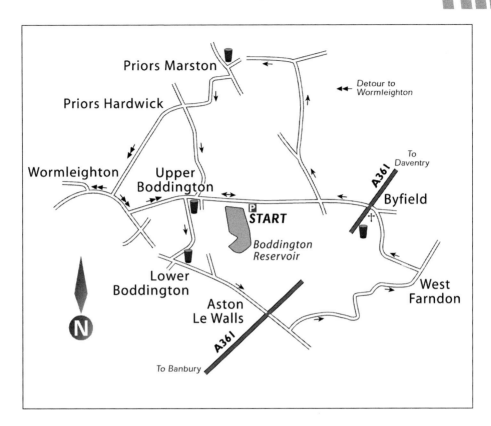

attractive village, once of much greater importance, with a pub and shop and a very steep high street.)

Very shortly, **turn L** (West Farndon). Keep on this road. Ignore the turn into West Farndon, and shortly **turn L** (Byfield/Daventry). The prominent spire of Byfield's church marks the way. At the mini-roundabouts on the A361, **turn L** at the first and immediately **turn R** at the second (Upper Boddington/Wormleighton). Byfield's shops and pub are to the left, along the A361.

At the crossroads on the edge of Byfield **turn R** (Priors Marston/Hellidon). *(Carry straight on at the crossroads to return to the reservoir.)* **Turn R** (Hellidon/Daventry), passing the prominent tower and masts. At the crossroads, **turn L** (Priors Marston/Southam). Enter Warwickshire. At the bottom of the steep hill **turn L** (Byfield/Priors Hardwick) and soon **turn R** (Priors Hardwick/Wormleighton). At the crossroads on the edge of Priors Hardwick **turn L** (Upper Boddington) and **turn L** again to return to the reservoir.

*To go to Wormleighton from Priors Hardwick, go straight on at the crossroads and continue through Priors Hardwick. At the T-junction, **turn R** (Wormleighton). In Wormleighton, **turn R** before the bus*

The route winds through the village of Byfield

*shelter, into a cul de sac, for the manor and church. On leaving, **turn L** to retrace your steps. Ignore the left turn for Priors Hardwick. Take the next left (Upper Boddington) shortly after. Follow this though the village and back to the car park at the reservoir.*

DROVE ROADS AND SHEEP IN NORTHAMPTONSHIRE

In the early part of the 19th century, around 15,000 cattle were fattened each year in Northamptonshire, before being sold at Smithfield Market in London. Cattle and sheep from Wales and the Borders and their drovers generally arrived along either Banbury Lane or The Welsh Road. Several stretches of modern road in the south-west of the county still bear these names. The Welsh Road entered the county near Upper Boddington and passed through Aston le Walls and on to Culworth, where it crossed Banbury Lane. Not only are the roads today better surfaced, they are less likely to be covered in the dung of fifteen thousand bovines. The potential for pasturing stock in this area had long been recognised, notably by John Spencer, who bought the manors of Upper and Lower Boddington in 1510, having earlier bought the manor at Althorp. That too was originally part of John Spencer's sheep grazing enterprise and, along with one based at Wormleighton and Boddington, gave the strong financial base on which the fortune of the Spencers was built. Wormleighton Manor, with its charming gatehouse, and church are hidden away in a cul de sac. For some, this peaceful spot might encapsulate the gentle delight of this part of the rural Midlands.

BODDINGTON POOL

The reservoir, now owned by the British Waterways Board, was built to provide water for the summit level of the Oxford and Coventry Canal. This linked the industrial Midlands to the river Thames. Before the building of the Grand Junction Canal (now the Grand Union Canal), it was the main route for manufactured goods on the way to London from the Midlands. The problem with any summit level of a canal was to keep enough water in it to enable boats to move. Reservoirs like this one were part of the solution. It is now popular with anglers and there is a nature reserve, too. It is pleasant to wander along the paths beside the water.

The far reaching view from Upper Boddington

17

Towcester and Sulgrave

17 miles (14 miles starting at Greens Norton) or
24 miles (21 miles, starting and finishing at Greens Norton)

Map: OS Landranger 152 Northampton and Milton Keynes (GR 692488)

Starting point: Start at the crossroads in the centre of Towcester, next to the Saracen's Head Hotel. Towcester is easily accessible from the A43 and A5. It is about 9 miles south-west of Northampton. Car parks are signposted, the most convenient for the start being off Northampton Road near the central crossroads in the town. Sulgrave or Greens Norton would make equally good starting points. The nearest railway stations are at Northampton and Wolverton, but both would add an extra 20 miles to the day!

Refreshments: There are a variety of cafés and pubs in Towcester, mostly along Watling Street: The Plough (01327 350738) is renowned for serving good value food. The Crown Inn at Weston (01295 760310) is good for food and drink. At Sulgrave there is a buttery for visitors to the Manor (see below), as well as the Star Inn (01295 760389), which serves good food, though it is wise to reserve a table if you wish to eat. Some village pubs have irregular hours, so check in advance if you are banking on a stop.

The route: Starting in the small town of Towcester, Lactodorum to the Romans, this ride, very much in England's heart, heads out to Sulgrave, with its celebrated ironstone manor house. This beautiful building was once the home of the Washington family, ancestors of George Washington. Along the way the route goes through the attractive villages of Greens Norton, Bradden and Weston. The village green at Abthorpe is especially attractive on a summer's evening. Returning to Towcester through Helmdon and Wappenham, this is typical rolling Northamptonshire countryside.

Start at the crossroads, where the A5 crosses Brackley Road/Northampton Road, at the Saracen's Head Hotel. Go along Brackley Road, signposted 'Council Offices' for ½ mile. At the roundabout take the **2nd exit**, immediately turning on to the cycle path to the traffic lights that aid the crossing of the A43 at the major roundabout ahead.

After crossing **keep R** and **turn L** (Abthorpe/Greens Norton). Soon **turn R** (Greens Norton). The manor was owned by the Greene family for six generations, the last owner dying in 1506. His sister, Matilda, was the mother of Catherine Parr, the wife who outlived Henry VIII. In the centre of Greens Norton **turn L** (Bradden/Slapton), immediately after

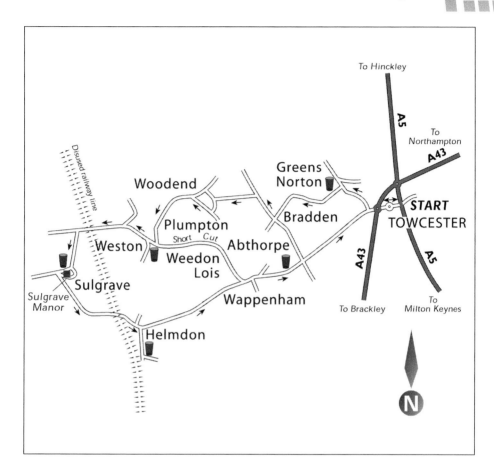

the butcher's shop. Follow this road through Bradden. At the T-junction, **turn R** (Blakesley).

After a mile, **turn L** (there is a signpost but no arm for the lane you should take) and cross a cattle grid a few yards ahead. There are good views from this road, which is the reason for taking it, and not to avoid Blakesley, which is in fact an attractive ironstone village. Should you miss this obscure turn, pick up the road for Woodend at the bottom of the hill. At the next T-junction **turn L** (Greens Park). Soon **turn R** (no signpost). This road is

often covered in mud and does not look promising. Eventually it emerges at a crossroads, near Rose Cottage, on the edge of Woodend. **Turn L** (no signpost).

Pass through Plumpton, with its neat manor house and church, until a T-junction is reached at Weston. **Turn R** (Weston/Culworth).

(A left turn at this junction will take you to Wappenham, on the main route. This will take you through Lois Weedon, where the road bends around the churchyard and a Norman ringwork to a little green, ideal

The church at Plumpton

for a picnic. This would make a complete circuit back to Towcester of about 17 miles.)

The main route passes through Weston and climbs gently out of the village. Cross the disused Grand Central Railway. The Grand Central Railway was the last mainline to be built and one of the first to be closed. A quarter of a mile later, **turn L** (no signpost) onto a narrow road. Follow the road downhill to a T-junction on a corner in Sulgrave. **Turn R**. Sulgrave Manor is on the left and the Star Inn is a little further up the street on the right.

At the next T-junction **turn L** (Helmdon). As you approach Helmdon you will get views of a viaduct that carried the Grand Central Railway over the valley and the disused Towcester to Banbury railway line. At the T-junction, by the war memorial, **turn L** (Wappenham).

The road rolls its way to Towcester passing through Wappenham and Abthorpe. Abthorpe's attractive green is reached by turning left in the village. To get back to the Towcester road, bear right into School Lane at the far end of the green. **Turn L** to resume your way to Towcester. As the big A43 roundabout comes into view, there is a left turn to Greens Norton. Take this if you started in that village. For Towcester, just carry on. It is best to use the bike crossing, as long as you end up going straight over and heading back down Brackley Road to the Saracen's Head.

TOWCESTER

Despite modern housing developments, Towcester is essentially still a linear town, stretched out along the A5, Watling Street. There is evidence of prehistoric settlement, but it was the Romans who established the first town. Lactodorum was one of a number of small military staging posts on the great road from London to Chester. The walls were repaired by King Edward the Elder between AD 917 and 921 when Towcester was a frontier town. Watling Street roughly marked the boundary between Saxon England and the Danelaw, controlled by Vikings. In the early 12th or late 11th century a motte and bailey castle was built: its grassy mound, the Bury Mount, is still clear on the northern side of Watling Street and Moat Lane. In the 15th century, William Sponne, a churchman who made money from rents on property in Towcester, established a grammar school. It was originally in the Chantry House, near the town hall, next to St Lawrence's church, where Sponne's tomb may be seen. The town was occupied during the English Civil War when Prince Rupert tried to use it as an advanced base against the Parliamentary stronghold of Northampton. The town prospered during the coaching age, the Saracen's Head is mentioned by Dickens in *The Pickwick Papers*, but there were several other coaching inns in the town, identifiable by their yards accessed under archways. There is a town trail, and a small museum is being developed to explain the history of this little town that reflects so much of England's past.

SULGRAVE

Sulgrave Manor is an excellent example of a 16th century manor house. It was built during a period when the gentry lived within the village – they would later build their mansions within extensive parkland, at some distance from the village. Keep your eyes open and you will see others, for example at Plumpton. Sulgrave's American connections begin with Lawrence Washington who bought the manor and sheep pasturage in 1539. His great-grandson, also Lawrence, went into the Church. However, he lost his living during the Civil War, when Parliament declared him to be a 'malignant Royalist'. His eldest son, John, migrated to America and established the Washington family there, and it was his great-grandson George who became the first president of the United States of America. There are guided tours around the manor as well as special events. The exterior of the manor is attractive, but the collection of furniture and artifacts from the 16th, 17th and 18th centuries is the real treasure, especially as many are displayed in position in rooms and not in glass cases. Information may be found on 01295 760205 or at www.sulgravemanor.org.uk.

The gable end dovecote, Sulgrave

18

Silverstone and Stowe

15 miles, 18 miles or 21 miles

A visit to one of the great country houses of England, a trip through an historic royal forest and a ride past the home of British motor racing: all here. Riding mostly on very minor roads, passing through gentle countryside with some extensive views, there are lots of surprises – especially around Dadford, Chackmore and Stowe Castle Farm. Lillingstone Dayrell and Lillingstone Lovell have the atmosphere of little forest villages, the latter with chocolate box buildings around the church. Stowe Landscape Gardens are a jewel of Georgian design and political propaganda, and the place where Lancelot 'Capability' Brown began his career and serious landscape gardening was born. Silverstone circuit, rapidly developing, brings this ride right up to date.

Map: OS Landranger 152 Northampton and Milton Keynes (GR 693447).

Starting point: The starting point, a little north of Whittlebury, is easily reached via the A43 and A413 near Towcester. There is a section of disused road ideal for parking at a road junction before reaching the village. If you start at Stowe Gardens, having used the National Trust car park there, remember that the gates are locked after closing time, so make sure you have time to complete your ride.

Refreshments: The Queen's Head in Chackmore (01280 813004) is a picturesque building with a garden. The Barley Mow (01327 811260), in Paulerspury, is convenient and friendly. In Silverstone, you will pass the White Horse (01327 858550), and a café at Stowe Landscape Gardens (see below) is available for those who pay the entrance fee.

The route: This area is best avoided when there is a Grand Prix at Silverstone. Except for a short section on the A413, which is not busy, the route is all on minor roads. There are few significant hills, though there are one or two short but sharp ones. The majority of this route is actually in Buckinghamshire. Buckingham is 1½ miles from Stowe and provides a full range of facilities.

Go south on the A413 towards Whittlebury. In Whittlebury, **turn R** into Church Way (Silverstone). At the mini-roundabouts in Silverstone **turn L** (Syresham) and immediately **turn R** (Village Centre). Keep left in the centre of the village to pass the White Horse and post office. At the crossroads, **turn R** (Syresham/Brackley). Keep left (All routes/Dadford/Stowe). A bridge takes you across the A43. Silverstone Circuit is on your left. Having undergone much redevelopment in recent years,

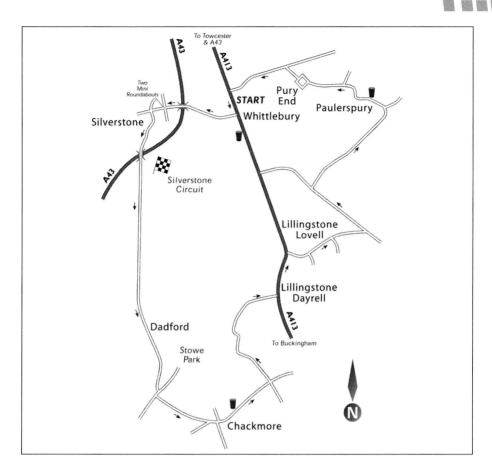

this is more than a racing circuit. There is a rally school and off-road course, amongst other things. It is also a centre for engineering, technology and design.

Having crossed the A43, you find yourself on a dual-carriageway, but you are unlikely to encounter much traffic. There is a series of roundabouts – keep straight on at all of them (Dadford/Stowe). Eventually the road becomes a country lane. As you approach Dadford you will see some of the monuments and the house at Stowe. About a mile after Dadford, the well-marked entrance to Stowe is on the left. The route carries straight on (Chackmore). **Turn L** (no signpost) immediately after passing a tarmac track leading to Stowe School, where the road you are on bears right towards Buckingham. Immediately enter Chackmore and reach the Queen's Head pub.

Pass through Chackmore. At the next crossroads, **turn L** (Lillingstone Dayrell/Towcester). Stowe Castle Farm is ahead. At the A413, with Lillingstone Dayrell church ahead across the fields, **turn L** (Towcester). The A413 is amongst the quietest of main roads,

The seat outside the church in Lillingstone Lovell makes an idyllic spot for a break

generally carrying very little traffic. If you wish to cut the route short, carry straight on along the A413 to Whittlebury.

For the main route, **turn R** (Lillingstone Lovell). The bench outside the church is an idyllic spot for a break. Carry on to a T-junction. **Turn L** (Paulerspury/Whittlebury). **Turn R** (no signpost) opposite a gate leading to some stables at the top of the long, but gentle ascent. *Carrying straight on at this point will take you back to the A413 where a right turn leads through Whittlebury to the start.*

On the main route, at the Paulerspury village sign, **turn L**, through the village. Paulerspury church has two medieval wooden funeral effigies. There are less than a hundred of these in England and Wales, ten in Northamptonshire. Another is nearby, in the church at Alderton.

Follow this road to Pury End. **Turn R** (Whittlebury). At the T-junction, **turn L** (Whittlebury), with roughly a mile to go to get back to the start.

● ●

STOWE LANDSCAPE GARDENS

Stowe House, Park and Landscape Gardens lie a couple of miles north-west of Buckingham. The house is now a school, but the gardens, which are in the care of the National Trust, are amongst the finest creations of the Georgian period. They are open from March to October on Wednesday, Thursday, Friday, Saturday and Sunday and at weekends only during the winter months. Telephone 01280 822850 (Monday to

Friday), 01280 818825 (weekends) or visit www.nationaltrust.org.uk. Last admission is 1½ hours before closing. This will give some idea of the extent of the gardens: there are lakes and 40 temples and monuments, amongst them the Temple of British Worthies. Free guided tours are available on most days. The House is undergoing restoration and is occasionally open under the auspices of the Stowe House Preservation Trust (telephone 01280 818166 for information).

WHITTLEWOOD FOREST

This route goes through what used to be Whittlewood Forest. This was one of the three main forests of Northamptonshire, the other two being Salcey and Rockingham. In the Middle Ages, forests were under the control of the monarch, partly to preserve the game for hunting and partly because they were potentially centres of disorder, being the haunt of outlaws. During the 18th and early 19th centuries, travellers were quite liable to be robbed as they went along what are now the A5 and A43. The forest was not all wooded: it was called forest because it came under Forest Law. Many people had rights to use the forest and its produce, but hunting was strictly forbidden without the monarch's permission. Amongst the monarchs who spent time here was Edward IV, who met Elizabeth Woodville near here: she searched him out to plead for her dead husband's lands to be returned to her. She ended up marrying Edward and gave birth to the boys who became the Princes in the Tower. It was near here, too, at Stony Stratford, that Richard, Duke of Gloucester, seized the princes from their Woodville and Hastings relatives, following the death of Edward IV.

The church of St James the Great, Paulerspury

(19)

Around St Rumbald's Well: King's Sutton

15 miles

In the Northamptonshire volume of *The King's England*, Arthur Mee quotes an old saying, 'Adderbury for strength, Bloxham for length, King's Sutton for beauty'. This refers to three church spires that are often visible on this ride. He goes on to say that King's Sutton church tower and spire is one of the 'glimpses of Northamptonshire that are not forgotten'. There are good views across the Cherwell, too, though the M40 has intruded on them in recent years. Middleton

---

Maps: OS Landranger 151 Stratford-upon-Avon (GR 405361) and 152 Northampton and Milton Keynes

Starting point: King's Sutton station. This is on the line between Oxford and Banbury. It is signposted in King's Sutton village, which is itself easily accessible from the A41 near Adderbury, south of Banbury. The route could also be started at Banbury station. Turn right on leaving the station approach, turn left at the first mini-roundabout and take the second exit at the next two mini-roundabouts, then follow the signs for Overthorpe. Parking is at a premium in King's Sutton, so try the large tree-lined green near the Memorial Hall. Middleton Cheney has more space for cars.

Refreshments: There are shops in King's Sutton and Middleton Cheney. The Marston Inn, at Marston St. Lawrence (01295 711906) serves good food and drink in pleasant surroundings and has a large beer garden. The White Horse in King's Sutton (01295 810843) is beautifully situated in a quiet corner of the village near the church. The village green in King's Sutton would be good for a picnic and there are several pretty wayside spots along the way.

The route: King's Sutton nestles in the valley of the River Cherwell. The route ascends gently through Overthorpe to Middleton Cheney, often with good views towards Oxfordshire. The A422 is crossed at Farthinghoe, and the return to King's Sutton is along quiet lanes with a speedy descent to take you back to the village. The entire route is on minor roads. The only place where heavy traffic is likely to be encountered is when crossing the A422 as it winds through Farthinghoe. Fortunately, there is a pedestrian crossing over which bikes can be pushed. As you would expect there are a few hills, but much of the route is pretty flat. This is not an easy route to cut short, though you might save a couple of miles by following signs to Middleton Cheney after King's Sutton.

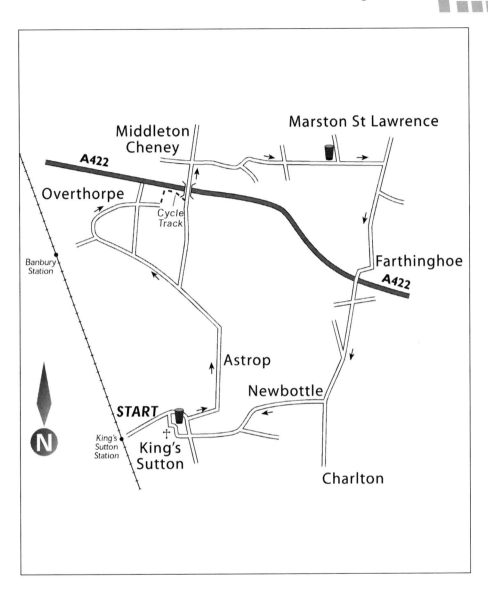

Cheney is a big village with shops; Marston St Lawrence is an idyllic place with a sleepy air redolent of lazy days; and Farthinghoe stands on a spur at the crossing of the A422. After Farthinghoe, a quiet lane brings a return to distant views, passing the isolated church at Newbottle. A little way south of King's Sutton is the attractive village of Aynho. Aynho Park was, until 1960, the home of the Cartwright family, frequently one of the two Northamptonshire County MPs, until the modern system of constituencies was set up. It is occasionally open to the public (telephone 01869 810636).

The unforgettable tower and spire of King's Sutton church

There is only one road from King's Sutton railway station. Take it. At the T-junction, **turn R** (Charlton/Aynho/Brackley). At the Three Tuns pub, **turn L** (Warkworth/Overthorpe). Follow this road out of the village past Astrop House and grounds, including St Rumbald's Well. Follow this road to Overthorpe.

Where the road bears sharp left for Banbury, **turn R** (Oxfordshire Cycleway: Middleton Cheney) into Overthorpe. Follow this to a crossroads. Go straight on (Home Farm/Middleton Cheney Cycle Route). This becomes a tarmac track alongside the A422. Watch out for the barriers. Carry on along this to the bridge ahead. At the bridge **turn L** to cross the A422 and soon to arrive at a crossroads by the war memorial in Middleton Cheney. **Turn R** (Farthinghoe/Brackley). In ½ mile, just before a garage and the New Inn, **turn L** (Thenford/Marston St Lawrence). Keep on this road to Marston St Lawrence. *If you want to go to the Marston Inn, follow the road into the village, wind past some attractive houses and the church and find the inn set back from the road on the left.*

The main route does not go into Marston St Lawrence. When the road swings sharp left, just before the village, **turn R** (no signpost, weight restriction). Cross an ornamental lake by a small stone bridge and proceed to a T-junction. **Turn R** (no signpost).

Follow this road up the hill and into Farthinghoe, with good views to the right. Keep left at the grassy triangle at the junction with the A422. Go almost straight on into Charlton Way (no signpost). Use the pedestrian crossing, if necessary. Very shortly, go straight on at the crossroads (Charlton/King's Sutton). Follow this road through some shady woodland. Before reaching Charlton, **turn R** (Newbottle/King's Sutton). Follow this road past the turning for Newbottle, with good views, through a pretty mixed wood to a T-junction. **Turn R** (King's Sutton). Now there is an exhilarating descent into King's Sutton – take care.

If you are returning to Overthorpe you may **turn R** before the large green and follow the signs. The main route keeps straight ahead, reaching a smaller green with the church ahead and the White Horse opposite it. Pass the church into a one-way street (Red Lion Street). At the junction keep on downhill (railway station).

ST RUMBALD AND KING'S SUTTON

St Rumbald (or St Rumbold, St Rumwold, St Rumwald) is not the best known of saints and no longer has a place in the official lists. He was the son of a king of Northumbria and a princess of Mercia, and he lived for just three days. However, in that short time, he is said to have cried out several times 'I am a Christian' and to have preached and quoted scripture. He is said to have been born at Sutton (hence King's Sutton), where there was something of a cult associated with the saint. King's Sutton is a pretty village and well worth exploring.

The isolated church at Newbottle nestles in woodland

20
Around Brackley

18 miles, 22 miles or 25 miles

Like Northampton, Brackley was once a royal borough. It prospered in the Middle Ages, and nowadays is a centre for the surrounding rural area. A very pleasant rural area it is, too. Brackley, a beautiful little town, is the best place to start and finish this ride, not only because it has the best facilities, but more so, because it has numerous old stone buildings that glow in the setting sun of a summer's evening. The countryside around Brackley provides peaceful cycling, with notable villages: the massive green at Evenley; little Mixbury; Westbury on the valley side; and Hinton-in-the-Hedges with its twisting lanes. This area is closely associated with Flora Thompson, whose autobiographical works, *Lark Rise*, *Over to Candleford* and *Candleford Green*, give such a vivid, if some say idealised, picture of rural life at the end of the 19th century. She was born in Juniper Hill, a hamlet a little way south of Evenley.

Map: OS Landranger 152 Northampton and Milton Keynes (GR 587370).

Starting point: There is plenty of parking in the market place in the centre of Brackley, and other parking in the town is signposted. Brackley is very easy to get to. The A43 and the A422 once met in the market place. The town now has a by-pass, so the lovely town centre is no longer choked by traffic. Evenley, signposted from the A43 south of Brackley, would make a good alternative start point.

Refreshments: The Crewe Arms at Hinton-in-the-Hedges (01280 705801), the Red Lion at Evenley (01280 703469) and the Reindeer at Westbury (01280 704934) are all worth a visit. The King's Head at Syresham is the last pub on route before returning to Brackley. Though the Bell Inn at Helmdon can easily be incorporated. In Brackley there are numerous pubs and places to get refreshment.

The route: The centre of Brackley can be busy, but once away from the town the traffic soon disappears, even if you chose to head straight for Evenley using the cycle track alongside the A43. There are main roads to cross and especial care should be taken at the busy roundabout on the A43 between Hinton-in-the-Hedges and Evenley, and you may find a lorry or two near the Brackley grain dryer, north of Westbury. From Syresham the route is on narrow lanes and then on a rough, but easily ridden, former road to Falcutt. A short stretch of minor, but potentially busy, road is encountered before the last few quiet miles to Brackley. It is difficult to find significant short cuts once you are out on this route without using several miles of the A422 or sections of the busy A43.

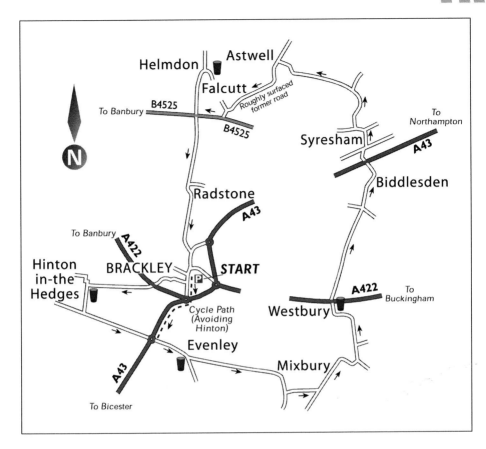

Go left out of the car park in the centre of Brackley, passing to the right of the town hall. At the T-junction **turn L** (All Other Routes). Towards the bottom of the hill, and using the filter lane, **turn R** (Hinton-in-the-Hedges: cyclists and pedestrians). This is a no-through-road to other traffic and is called Hinton Road. If you are not confident about crossing a busy dual-carriageway at a roundabout, I recommend a short there-and-back ride to Hinton-in-the-Hedges following the directions below.

(At this point you could make straight for Evenley, to complete a circuit of 18 miles and miss out the roundabout on the A43.

To do this do not turn for Hinton-in-the-Hedges, but instead keep straight on to pick up the cycle track signposted Evenley. This goes straight on at two roundabouts and uses a cycle track next to the A43 as far as the roundabout.)

Having turned right for Hinton-in-the-Hedges, keep ahead past a attractive lake on the right – public access, bench seats, etc – pass through two barriers, with gaps for cycles, to reach the A422. Go straight over (Hinton-in-the-Hedges) and follow this narrow lane through the village, signposted Evenley, passing the well-shaded green and the well-hidden Crewe Arms. At

Astwell Castle Farm and the surrounding countryside

the crossroads, **turn L** (no sign at present, but towards Evenley). Follow this straight road to the A43 and cross with care. *(This potentially busy crossing can be avoided by following the cycle-track out of Brackley and ignoring Hinton-in-the Hedges.)* On the far side you meet the cycle track that comes directly from Brackley. Before long, enter Evenley and emerge on the extensive village green. **Turn R** (no signpost). There is a village shop on the opposite side of the green.

Pass the Red Lion and keep straight-ahead (Mixbury). In Mixbury, **turn L** (no signpost) just before the church. At the T-junction, **turn L** (Westbury), immediately crossing over a disused railway line. At the next T-junction, **turn L** again (Westbury). As Westbury is approached, follow the Village Only signs as the road swings to the left. Continue up Main Street to a crossroads near the Reindeer public house. Cross straight over (Biddlesden/Syresham). Nearly 2 miles later go straight on and a few yards later **turn L** (Biddlesden). The signpost here is often pointing incorrectly towards Whitfield.

Pass through Biddlesden and shortly after crossing the bridge over the A43 **turn R** (Northampton/Syresham) and immediately **turn L** (Syresham and Wappenham). Pass the King's Head and opposite the school, **turn R** (Astwell/Wappenham). Follow this road as it winds out of Syresham, passing a broad verge with a pleasant bench for a sunny day. When the road bears right, **turn L** (Helmdon). After a while the battlements of Astwell Castle Farm come into view.

At the T-junction **turn L** (Astwell). This starts as a surfaced road but becomes rough. However, the surface is

sound and it is a good ride even after heavy rain. Ignore the turn to Falcutt Barn, keeping straight on to eventually reach a small tarmac lane. **Turn L** (no signpost). Very soon, at a T-junction, **turn L** (Crowfield/Syresham).

(At this point a right turn, signposted Helmdon, will take you to the Bell Inn. At the T-junction, a left turn will take you to the crossroads to rejoin the main route. It is a mile longer than the B road and the hill from Helmdon is unremitting, but it does avoid the half mile of rat run.)

Turn R (Helmdon/Middleton Cheney B4525). This can be surprisingly busy. Fortunately in less than ½ mile **turn L** (Brackley) at a crossroads immediately after a bridge over the disused Grand Central Railway.

This road is followed all the way back to the edge of Brackley. On reaching the housing estate, **turn R** (Brackley) at a T-junction and, shortly, **turn R** (Brackley). At the next T-junction **turn R** (no signpost) and follow this road back to the centre of Brackley.

● ●

BRACKLEY

Brackley was an important place in the Middle Ages. In 1215 a group of barons met in the castle, sending their demands to King John, who was at Oxford. King John refused them, but it was only a matter of time before he was forced to agree to Magna Carta. A few years later, Brackley Castle, of which nothing remains, witnessed arbitration between Henry III and rebellious barons led by Simon de Montfort. A Royal Charter was granted to Brackley in 1235, and later the town became an important market for sheep and the wool trade. In 1447 William Waynfleete founded Magdalen

College School. It seems that he was keen that scholars from Magdalen College Oxford have somewhere to go to escape bouts of plague that afflicted the university. By the end of the 17th century, the town's affluence was in decline, along with the wool trade. However, it passed into the hands of the Duke of Bridgewater, who provided the prominent town hall in 1707. He also controlled the two parliamentary seats that went with Brackley's status as a Royal Borough. Today, the long broad main street is lined with trees and buildings that remind us of a long and prosperous past. Waynfleete's buildings are still there, though somewhat altered from the Tudor and Stuart period. There are various places to eat and drink, which may be more immediately useful at the end of the ride.